teen's
guides

LIVING
with
OBESITY

teen's guides

LIVING
with
OBESITY

Nicolas Stettler, M.D., M.S.C.E.
with Susan Shelly

☑️ Checkmark Books®
An imprint of Infobase Publishing

Living with Obesity

Checkmark Books
An imprint of Facts On File, Inc.
132 West 31st Street
New York NY 10001

Library of Congress Cataloging-in-Publication Data

Stettler, Nicolas.
  Living with obesity / by Nicolas Stettler with Susan Shelly.
    p. cm. — (Teen's guides)
  Includes bibliographical references and index.
  ISBN-13: 978-0-8160-7590-4 (hardcover : alk. paper)
  ISBN-10: 0-8160-7590-5 (hardcover : alk. paper)
  ISBN-13: 978-0-8160-7591-1 (pbk : alk. paper)
  ISBN-10: 0-8160-7591-3 (pbk : alk. paper)
 1. Obesity in adolescence. 2. Obesity. I. Shelly, Susan. II. Title.
RJ399.C6S74 2009
616.3'9800835—dc22   2008046579

Checkmark Books are available at special discounts when purchased in bulk quantities for businesses, associations, institutions or sales promotions. Please call our Special Sales Department in New York at (212) 967-8800 or (800) 322-8755.

You can find Facts On File on the World Wide Web at http://www.factsonfile.com

Text design by Annie O'Donnell
Cover design by Jooyoung An

Printed in the United States of America

MP Hermitage 10 9 8 7 6 5 4 3 2 1

This book is printed on acid-free paper.

Disclaimer
Case studies presented in this book are based on or composites of stories of children who are not patients of Dr. Nicolas Stettler. Names and details have been altered to protect the privacy of various individuals.

CONTENTS

A NOTE FROM THE AUTHORS

This book is written for you and teens like you, so your feedback is very important to everyone who worked on it. Please e-mail your comments and suggestions about this book to livingwithobesity@gmail.com. Let us know what you liked or didn't like about this book, what we might have forgotten to discuss, and what else you would like to learn in a book about obesity. Tell us if this book has helped you in one way or another, and what we could have done better for you. Thanks for your time.

ACKNOWLEDGMENTS

The authors would like to thank the following colleagues who contributed their time and expertise to this book: Lara Khouri, program director, Healthy Weight Program, the Children's Hospital of Philadelphia; Todd J. Levy, OTR/L, CBIST, occupational therapist, the Children's Hospital of Philadelphia; and Myles Faith, Ph.D., assistant professor of psychology in psychiatry, the University of Pennsylvania.

Dr. Stettler also would like to thank his mentors, teachers, patients and their parents, as well as family and friends without whom this book would not have been possible.

What Is Obesity?

You can hardly open a newspaper or magazine or turn on the TV without coming across an article or program about *obesity*. We read and hear about the obesity epidemic—obesity in adults, obesity in adolescents and teens, the associated problems of obesity, and the latest treatments for obesity. Exactly what, however, is obesity?

You can find a lot of different definitions, but basically, obesity is simply an excess of body fat that is associated with health problems.

While the definition of obesity is simple and straightforward, the issues surrounding it are a little more complicated. Obesity can contribute to a variety of diseases and conditions, and can affect you not only physically, but also socially and psychologically.

In this chapter, we'll take a closer look at overweight and obesity, how they are determined, and how they might be affecting your life.

HOW DO I KNOW IF I'M OBESE?

It might seem that it would be easy to figure out if someone is obese, but that's not always the case. Determining whether a person is overweight or obese can be difficult, and not everyone is in agreement as to how that determination should be made. Generally, though, *body mass index,* or BMI, is used to determine whether a teenager is at a healthy weight, or is overweight or obese.

BMI is a number that's calculated from your height and weight, and then plotted on a chart in order to get a percentile ranking. That is, your BMI is compared to a reference group of teenagers of the same age and gender as you. If your BMI, which reflects both your weight and your height, is higher than that of most other people of the same age and gender, you're considered to be overweight or obese.

There's been ongoing debate about how to classify teenagers regarding weight, and what terms to use when doing so, and that has resulted in some confusion. For the purposes of this book, we'll use the following guidelines:

> If your BMI is greater than 85 percent, but less than 95 percent, of others of the same sex and age, you're described as overweight.
> If your BMI is greater than that of 95 percent of others of the same sex and age, you're described as obese.

These classifications are useful for health professionals because they help them decide what to recommend to their patients. They are not meant, however, to put people into boxes or be judgmental. Every individual and every culture has different view of what obesity means, and some may consider these terms offensive. We use them here in the medical context as they help describe and understand the issues related to excessive body fat. Additionally, BMI is not a perfect science, and two people with the same BMI can look and feel very different. And, BMI doesn't actually measure body fat and the negative health conditions associated with fat, so it's possible that someone can have a relatively high BMI that would classify him or her as obese, but doesn't have excessive fat and therefore is not obese. The other way around also is possible. So, while BMI is used as an indicator of overweight and obesity, it shouldn't be thought of as perfect, but rather as a screening tool to alert a health professional to look into excessive fat and health complications.

Both the Centers for Disease Control and Prevention (CDC), a branch of the U.S. Department of Health and Human Services, and the American Academy of Pediatrics recommend BMI as an indicator of overweight or obesity for children, adolescents, and teenagers. If you want to check your BMI, you can access the CDC's BMI calculator at apps.nccd.cdc.gov/dnpabmi/Calculator.aspx. It's easy to use, and can give you an idea of the percentile in which you fall, according to your age, height, and weight.

Be aware, however, that the CDC uses different terms when classifying teens according to BMI. While we classify those with a BMI of

It's easy in our society to become overly concerned about your weight and your appearance in general. We are, after all, bombarded constantly with advertisements for products that promise to help us look thinner, and therefore, make us happier. It's nearly impossible to ignore the constant messages that thin is beautiful, and should be achieved at any cost. It's important to remember, however, that not everyone who is thin is beautiful, and many overweight and obese people are beautiful, especially when they are comfortable with themselves and confident.

Happiness comes in all sizes and shapes, to be sure. The concern over obesity isn't about how an obese person looks, but about the health problems that often accompany the condition.

more than 85 but less than 95 percent of others in the same sex and age group as overweight, the CDC calls that group "at risk of overweight."

And, while we classify those with a BMI of more than 95 percent of others of the same sex and age as obese, the CDC calls that group "overweight."

Despite the differences in language, the calculator will still help you to gauge your BMI and give you an idea of where you fall on the charts. If you have questions regarding your weight, however, you should consult your family doctor or a nutritionist.

THE INCREASING OCCURRENCE OF OVERWEIGHT AND OBESITY IN TEENAGERS

Statistics vary, depending on the source, but there's no question that obesity among teens is far more common than it used to be. The CDC tells us that the obesity rate among adolescents and teens in the United States has tripled since 1980. More than 9 million young people between the ages of six and 19 are considered overweight or obese—about 17 percent of that population, according to the National Institutes of Health.

While this book will concentrate on overweight and obesity among American teens, overweight and obesity are by no means confined to the United States. While obesity was once considered to be a problem only in affluent countries, now even middle- and low-income countries are being affected, particularly in urban settings, according to the World Health Organization, which operates within the United Nations system. This creates a terrible problem for poor countries with very limited resources already struggling with health problems caused by disease and insufficient nutrition. It's not easy to understand, but obesity can occur side by side with undernutrition.

The increasing problems of overweight and obesity are occurring throughout the world and affecting all ages. Health professionals around the world are concerned, and trying to figure out why the problems of overweight and obesity are increasing, and what can be done to solve them.

You'll learn a lot more about causes for obesity in chapter 2, so we won't spend a lot of time here exploring those. It's safe to say, however, that there are some reasons for the increase in obesity: an increased availability of high-calorie foods, coupled with changes in our lifestyles that compel us to expend less *energy*.

IS OBESITY A DISEASE?

Just as there are disagreements about how obesity should be determined and defined, the question of whether obesity is a disease is a topic of controversy. There are a wide range of views and opinions from doctors, insurance and drug companies, scientists, and the public over whether obesity is a disease in itself, or a condition that contributes to diseases.

The Internal Revenue Service in 2002 designated obesity a disease so that taxpayers could deduct medical costs associated with weight loss. And in 2004 the Centers for Medicare and Medicaid Services came a step closer to having obesity categorized as a disease when it changed a policy that had prevented obese people from getting coverage to pay for weight-loss therapies such as surgery, medications, counseling, and nutrition education.

While the policy change didn't guarantee these benefits for everyone enrolled in the Medicare and *Medicaid* programs, it opened the door for some services, and encouraged more serious discussion about how obesity should be classified and treated.

Private insurance companies, however, are balking at picking up costs for health interventions to treat or prevent obesity, such as *gastric bypass surgery*, and there is ongoing debate over whether that and other treatments should be covered by health insurance.

People who favor classifying obesity as a disease argue that it will aid people who are currently unable to get treatment for their conditions, will encourage people to seek help, and will reduce the stigma often associated with being obese or overweight. People opposed to calling obesity a disease claim it will detract from the treatment of other serious diseases, and that obesity is best left for individuals to deal with.

While there is little argument that obesity contributes to a variety of ailments including heart disease, *diabetes,* sleep disorders, *high blood pressure,* breathing problems, and even cancer, the debate remains over whether obesity is a disease in its own right.

Whether or not obesity is categorized as a disease, however, shouldn't influence how you feel about your weight or your health care. If you're concerned about your weight or related health condition, you need to seek advice from a doctor or other qualified health care professional.

DETERMINING WHETHER YOUR WEIGHT IS A PROBLEM

If you find yourself wheezing or having trouble catching your breath as you climb stairs, or you've been diagnosed with high blood pressure or high levels of *triglycerides,* or you feel sleepy during the day, you may be experiencing medical problems associated with obesity.

While many of the serious diseases associated with obesity typically don't show up until adulthood, there are a variety of health problems that can affect teenagers and young adults. As more and more Americans are becoming obese at increasingly early ages, we're seeing serious illness, including diabetes and even sudden death, occur in teenagers.

You'll read much more about the physical effects of obesity in chapter 4, but listed below are some illnesses and medical disorders that are becoming more common among teens who are overweight or obese.

- ➤ Arthritis
- ➤ Blount's disease
- ➤ Breathing problems
- ➤ Fatty liver
- ➤ Gallstones
- ➤ Type 2 diabetes
- ➤ Hypertension
- ➤ Increased blood lipid levels, including high cholesterol and triglycerides

> Polycystic ovary syndrome (PCOS)
> Sleeping problems
> Slipped capital femoral epiphyses (SCFE)

You'll read throughout this book about the importance of making small changes to improve your health. While it's probably unrealistic or even dangerous to decide to lose 50 or 60 pounds in the next three months, it may be completely realistic to decide to take your dog for a 20-minute walk every day or to switch from drinking soda to water. Many medical issues or potential medical problems can be prevented or improved by making small changes that soon become habits, even if you remain overweight!

Meanwhile, if you're concerned that you're experiencing weight-related medical problems—or any medical problems, for that matter—talk to a parent or other adult about getting you an appointment with a doctor.

Unfortunately, being overweight or obese can affect more than your physical health. It can affect your overall quality of life as well. A study conducted in 2003 revealed that kids and teens who were obese experienced a lower overall quality of life than those who weren't obese. In fact, the quality of life for obese kids and teens was comparable to that of kids and teens with cancer.

TV shows like *The Biggest Loser* and *Shaq's Big Challenge* are classified as reality shows, but they actually contain very little reality. What would be far more realistic is to follow the "winners" of those shows for several years to see who, if anyone, keeps the weight off. Rapid, extreme weight loss often results in *weight cycling,* which is an undesirable process of losing, gaining, losing, and gaining weight. Making heroes of people who lose weight under completely artificial circumstances only perpetuates the myth that all you need is a little willpower and the extra weight will melt away. The truth is that it's hard to lose weight, and harder to keep it off once you've lost it. It's also true that you don't have to be "the biggest loser" to improve your health by losing even small amounts of weight and working to be as healthy as possible.

Clearly, obesity has negative effects, both medically and in other areas, as well. Chapter 4 explores how being obese affects you physically, psychologically, and socially, so you'll read a lot more about this topic then.

What you need to understand, though, is that, to some extent, obesity does, or will, affect your life in a negative manner. At some point it's likely that you'll experience health problems related to your weight, or you won't get a job that you really wanted because the person hiring is prejudiced against those who are overweight, or you'll make excuses to skip a trip to the beach with your friends because you don't want to be seen in a bathing suit.

If you've already experienced those or similar problems, or anticipate that you may experience them, don't be overly discouraged. There are lots of things you can do to assure that you'll grow up as healthy and happy as you can be, no matter how much you weigh.

WHERE TO LOOK FOR HELP AND SUPPORT

One thing is for certain: There is no shortage of advice out there for teens who are concerned about their weight. You can find promises of miracle diets, pills that melt off pounds, and supplements that will change your body *metabolism* and your life. Magazines contain articles as well as advertisements regarding weight loss, and the Internet is cluttered with information, products, and advice. If what you see on the Internet is true, you'll be able to find the ideal exercise program for your body type (guaranteed to help you lose 10 pounds the very first week!), a miracle tea that will result in dramatic weight lost instantly, and other products to help you quickly and easily lose weight.

The problem, of course, is figuring out what's true and what's not true, and even more importantly, what's safe and what's not safe. Do a search for "weight loss products" and you'll see listings for all sorts of diet aids, including an organic weight loss supplement made from wild American herbs. Supplements such as that are not helpful, and can be extremely dangerous. When looking for advice and help concerning your weight, it's extremely important that you rely on dependable sources, such as your family doctor or school nurse.

Remember that there are many people trying to cash in on what's become known as the obesity epidemic. Don't ever buy or accept any medicines or other weight loss–related products from anyone other than your doctor. Listed below are some reliable sources that you should be able to consult about issues related to your weight.

Your family doctor. Your family doctor can work with you regarding your weight, or refer you to another doctor or medical care provider who specializes in teen obesity. If you don't have or can't afford a family doctor, you may be able to receive medical care at a clinic or community health center in your area.

A *registered dietician or nutritionist*. A registered dietician or nutritionist can be very helpful in educating you about nutrition, appropriate *portion* sizes, fat and *calorie* contents of different foods, and other subjects. If you are referred by your doctor to a nutritionist, some or all of the costs may be covered by insurance. Also, hospitals sometimes offer health fairs or seminars regarding nutrition that you might find useful.

A *counselor*. A counselor may be a valuable resource if you feel that you're suffering from *depression* or other disorders. If you don't have access to a private counselor, ask to make an appointment with the guidance counselor at your school.

Your school nurse. Your school nurse should be able to answer your questions regarding overweight and obesity, and may be able to direct you to further information or help.

A *community organization*. A community organization such as the YMCA or a Boys & Girls Club may have resources to help you get more information and support.

Friends and family members. Friends and family members can be sources of support, but remember that they are likely to be emotionally involved with you and your feelings, and perhaps not able to offer you the objective advice and guidance that a professional counselor or school nurse could. Your mother, for instance, might be tempted to remind you about the candy wrappers she found in your room, setting off another round of arguments, accusations, and frustration.

Outside sources, such as books, magazines, and the Internet. Outside sources like books, magazines, and the Internet contain some very good and reliable information. The problem, as mentioned above, is sorting out the useful information from that which is useless—and even potentially harmful.

As you know, there are hundreds and hundreds of Web sites dealing with weight control and obesity, so it's important to know which ones are considered to be reliable and safe. Generally, Web sites posted by the government (with addresses ending in ".gov") are considered to be reliable, as are most of those of colleges and universities (with addresses ending in ".edu"). Just be careful not to confuse student sites with the institutional sites—both can have Web addresses ending in "edu."

Some Web sites posted by nonprofit organizations can be considered pretty reliable, although if the organization is an advocacy group or represents the interest of the food industry or other private for-profit organization, the information is likely biased. Most of those nonprofit sites' addresses end in ".org."

Some examples of Web sites that are considered to contain valuable and reliable information regarding obesity for teens are: www. medlineplus.gov, a consumer health database compiled by the National Library of Medicine; www.cdc.gov, the site of the Centers for Disease Control and Prevention; www.americanheart.org, hosted by the American Heart Association; and www.obesity.org, the site of the Obesity Society. You'll find lots more recommended Web sites listed in the appendix, but these can help to get you started.

KNOWING THAT YOU'RE NOT ALONE

The teen years aren't easy, and hardly anyone comes out of them completely unscathed. Being a teenager is hard work, with pressure coming at you from all sides, even from within yourself. You probably feel pressured by your parents, your teachers, and your friends. And our culture imposes a great deal of pressure by perpetuating the ideas that you're supposed to be smart and pretty and popular, wear the latest styles of clothing, and always be happy.

It might be hard for you to believe, but all teens—even those that you might think have perfect lives—face the same pressures that you do. Teenagers are notoriously hard on themselves, and very few are completely satisfied with how they look and act and with what they accomplish.

For those struggling with overweight or obesity, however, the teen years can be even more difficult. Despite the fact that more and more people—kids, teens, and adults—are becoming obese, our society continues to hold up thinness, even extreme thinness, as the ideal. This can result in an ongoing sense of failure for those who don't conform to the images you see in magazines and on television and the Internet.

Overweight and obese teens often suffer from feelings of isolation and disappointment in themselves and others. Some live in constant fear of being bullied or ridiculed about their weight. Teens who blog on weight-related Web sites leave comments such as, "There were times I just wished I could disappear and never come back," and "I just wish I could be healthy and not a big couch potato." A 27-year-old recalling her high school days shared this: "I still remember (like it was yesterday) how terrible I felt every day of my life. I never felt good enough. I used to go to bed at night wishing and praying that I would just wake up thin."

The point of sharing these comments is to let you know that you're not alone, and that you have the potential to improve your situation. Remember what you read a little earlier about making small changes to improve your health? Taking charge and making even small changes will help you to feel more in control of your life, and that's empowering.

If you're concerned about your weight, you've already taken a very positive step by picking up this book. You'll learn a lot more about taking control of your weight—and your life—as you continuing reading.

WHAT YOU NEED TO KNOW

- ➤ Obesity is defined simply as an excess of body fat that is associated with health problems.
- ➤ Body mass index (BMI) is the most common standard used to determine overweight or obesity in teenagers.
- ➤ The prevalence of obesity among teenagers has tripled since 1980, according to the Centers for Disease Control and Prevention.
- ➤ Many reasons contribute to the increase in obesity, including an increased availability of high-calorie foods and lifestyles that cause us to expend less energy.
- ➤ Debate is ongoing as to whether obesity is a disease in itself or a condition that contributes to other diseases, such as diabetes and heart disease.

➤ Obesity can affect your physical health, and also impacts negatively on your overall quality of life.
➤ You can identify reliable sources to go to for help and advice regarding your weight.
➤ Making just small lifestyle changes can positively affect your health and make you feel more in charge of your life even without losing lots of weight at once.

2

What Causes Obesity?

Eating too much fast food and junk food, drinking too many sodas, and spending too much time in front of the television and the computer are often cited as primary reasons for an increase in teen overweight and obesity. And clearly, these factors seem to contribute to the problem.

While they're easy targets for blame, there are a variety of factors that contribute to weight, some of which are much more complicated than cheeseburgers and video games.

In this chapter, we'll examine some causes or underlying risk factors for the development of obesity, and look at why some people become overweight or obese while others don't.

UNDERSTANDING ENERGY BALANCE

In order to understand why people lose and gain weight, you'll need to be familiar with the concepts of energy and *energy balance.* "Energy," as it's used here, refers to calories. We often think of energy as something that gives us pep and makes us feel more awake, such as coffee or an energy drink. You've probably heard someone say, "I need some energy," as they drink some juice or coffee. Using the word "energy" in that context refers to something that is stimulating, or that wakes you up. For the purposes of this discussion, however, energy refers to the calories contained in what we eat and drink.

The calories you consume, whether they're in your breakfast cereal, an apple, ice cream, or a steak, power your body to do what you need to do. Calories give you the energy necessary to get up, get to school, participate in extracurricular activities, get back home, and hang out with your friends. A calorie is a unit of measurement for energy. You need a certain number of calories in order to do all those things mentioned above, because when you perform activities, you burn off, or use up, the energy those calories provide.

Even when you're not actively engaging in activity, your body is expending energy and burning up calories. It takes energy just to stay alive, whether you're stretched out in your bed or playing basketball.

As an adolescent or teenager, your body is still growing and changing, which in itself requires energy. So, as you can see, it's extremely important that you get enough energy, or calories, to allow your body to not only function, but to grow and thrive.

When you consume about as many calories as you use up to stay alive, grow, and participate in daily activities, it's called energy balance. You're expending about as many calories as you're consuming. If you consume many more calories than you use, or use up many more calories than you consume, that's called *energy imbalance.*

To figure out energy balance and imbalance as it pertains to you, it's important to have an idea of the number of calories you consume over a period of a few days, and how much energy you use up during the same amount of time. That way, you can figure out what are the important components of *energy intake* and *energy expenditure* in your own life. Some people tend to burn off calories more quickly than others, so you could consume the same number of calories as your friend, but if your body burns less than her body does—for example, if your body is smaller or if you engage in less physical activity than she does—she may end up with energy balance while you do not.

Keeping track of your energy intake and expenditure for a few days may help you to get a better sense of how your body is using the calories you consume, but you have to understand that you'll never be able to track energy intake and expenditure precisely enough to determine exact energy balance or imbalance. Many people monitor their dietary intake as part of a weight loss program, but that's a different situation than keeping track for a few days to get a better idea of your energy intake and expenditure. There are lots of charts and graphs that provide the calorie contents of common foods, and the number of calories expended during a variety of activities. These can help you to get a better idea of how many calories you're taking in and burning off. A good one to check out is the U.S. Department of Agriculture's MyPyramid Tracker (www.mypyramidtracker.gov), an interactive tool that analyzes energy balance based on entries of foods you've eaten and activities performed.

According to the National Institutes of Health, consuming just 150 more calories a day than you use up in activity will result in a weight gain of 10 pounds over a year, 20 pounds over two years, and so on. On the flip side, to lose 10 pounds in a year, you only have to eliminate 150 calories a day.

To give you an idea of how that information translates to real life, consider this: A 12-ounce can of soda contains about 150 calories. So do each of the following: four Girl Scout Thin Mint cookies, a half cup of vanilla ice cream, or a hot dog without the roll.

People sometimes get caught up trying to figure out if they're overweight or obese because they consume too many calories, or because they don't get enough exercise to expend the calories they eat. In truth, it's not one factor or another, because each factor is dependent on the other. It's the energy imbalance that causes obesity, not the act of consuming too many calories or burning off too few.

It's very difficult to measure exactly how much energy you're taking in, and how much you're expending, and you'll drive yourself crazy if you try to achieve perfect energy balance every day. Energy balance occurs over a period of several days, and it's not an exact science. Most people don't achieve energy balance every day; it occurs over a period of time.

As you read in chapter 1, and will read throughout this book, small lifestyle changes can result in significant improvements to your health

When you were a kid, did you ever try to play on a seesaw with someone who weighed either a lot more or a lot less than you did? Remember what happened? You couldn't play, because one of you weighed more than the other and you couldn't get the seesaw to balance. It wasn't your fault or your friend's fault that the seesaw wouldn't balance, it was just that you were two different sizes. That's how it is with energy consumption and expenditure. It not that there's too much or too little of either; it's just that, when obesity occurs, it shows that there isn't proper balance between the two.

and well-being. Substituting an apple for the chocolate chip cookies, and walking to a friend's house instead of driving or getting a ride, can help you to move closer to achieving energy balance—or even to burning off more calories than you consume, which would result in weight loss.

MANY CAUSES, MANY QUESTIONS

Just as with other health conditions, there are many factors that can contribute to obesity. Some of these factors are genetic, environmental, hereditary, and metabolic. *Eating disorders,* such as night eating or bulimia, can be related to obesity, as can the use of certain medications, such as steroids or cancer chemotherapy. Cultural factors also can contribute to obesity. In fact, the causes for obesity, or for being at risk for obesity, are complex, and largely dependent on the culture and environment in which a person lives.

Scientists and doctors are learning more all the time about obesity and its causes, but many questions still remain. While what and how much individuals eat used to be considered pretty much the sole reason for overweight and obesity, and certainly is known to be a factor, we're recognizing many additional reasons why so many people have trouble achieving and maintaining healthy weights.

One of the factors that is relatively clear is the body's tendency to return to its former weight status. If, for instance, you weight 220 pounds and you lose 30 pounds, the tendency of your body is to regain the weight lost. This is thought to be the result of the programming of the human body over thousands and thousands of years to maintain weight in order to avoid starvation.

It's thought that centuries ago, humans who were able to regain the weight they had lost during a famine were more likely to stay alive during the next famine than those who didn't. They were also more likely to stay alive to have children and pass on these "good genes" to the next generation. As you can imagine, over time, more and more people had these good or survival genes and they progressively became universal to all human beings. In other words, over time, the human body adapted to hold onto weight as a survival method. The problem is that today, when most people are not exposed to repeated famines, these "good genes" for survival are not much help anymore, and they make it very difficult to lose weight.

If you dramatically reduce the number of calories you consume, your body will "turn itself down" by slowing activity and lowering metabolism, and will stimulate appetite in a way that is difficult to overcome. This makes it very difficult to keep weight off, because despite your best efforts to make it do otherwise, your body, which still believes that there is a famine coming up soon, is working hard to stay at, or return to, its former weight. This tendency for your body to want to return to a former weight is sometimes called the set point theory. That is, your body has a natural point of stability when it comes to weight, so if you gain or lose weight, your body will work to return to that natural point.

While many researchers support the set point theory, not everyone agrees. There are many different viewpoints and opinions regarding the causes of obesity, some of which have greater credibility than others. In recent years, reports have emerged blaming obesity on numerous factors, some considered by health professionals to be dubious at best. Common sense tells us there is no single reason that people become obese, but that obesity is caused by a combination of factors, some of which are more controllable than others.

BIOLOGICAL AND GENETIC COMPONENTS OF OBESITY

There is significant evidence indicating that *genes* play an important role in a person's tendency to become obese, and that overweight and obesity run in families. Studies have shown that children adopted when they are very young tend to develop body weights similar to their birth parents, not their adoptive parents. And identical twins, who share genetic makeup, tend to be much more similar in body weights than fraternal twins, who do not have all the same genes, but live in the same family and environment the way identical twins do.

If you want to determine whether or not you're biologically predisposed to obesity, just take a look at other members of your family. If your parents and their parents are overweight or obese, your chances of obesity are greater than if they are not.

Researchers believe there are probably a number of genes that are related to weight. There may be genes that affect how people process food, and even why some people desire to eat more than others. Genes may play a role in determining energy balance by controlling a person's metabolism, which is the process the body uses to convert food to energy, or by signaling how much we need to eat before we feel full. It may be that genes even help to determine how active a person will be. In short, there are a large number of genes that can contribute to obesity and it is very unlikely that one single gene will be discovered that determines with certainty if someone will become obese or not. This also makes it very unlikely that cutting-edge scientific discoveries and progresses, such as gene therapy, will ever be a solution to the obesity problem in our society, because so many genes would have to be changed at the same time. In other words, unfortunately, *genetics* is not the "magic bullet" that will cure obesity.

AM I DOOMED TO BECOME OBESE?

While it's pretty much agreed upon that genetics play an important role in whether someone will become obese, and that a person with obese parents or grandparents is at increased risk for obesity, it is not a done deal that every child or teen with obesity in his or her family will become obese. On the other hand, for various reasons, some children and teens whose parents are of healthy weight do become obese.

While members of immediate families share genetic traits, they also tend to share a lot of other characteristics, such as exercise habits, food choices, living environments, and other lifestyle features. Even if they are not exactly the same, chances are good that over your life, the foods you eat and the activities you participate in will be more similar to those of other members of your own family than to those of other families. If those things contribute to obesity in one family member, chances are that they will do the same for other family members as well. In other words, genetics, which you can't change, is not the only thing that makes people in a family similar in weight status. There are other contributing factors that you can change as an individual to decrease your risk of becoming obese or the severity of your obesity if you are already obese.

There's a saying that goes, "Genetics loads the gun, but the environment pulls the trigger." This means that while some people are genetically predisposed to obesity, it's likely that they also live in environments that encourage obesity. You'll read much more about environmental causes for obesity in the next chapter.

While you can't control the genes that you've inherited, there are factors that you can control that may make a difference in your weight. If you suspect that you're predisposed toward obesity because of your genes, you shouldn't be discouraged. Take it as a signal to be proactive and begin making some healthy changes in your lifestyle and environment. If you see a lot of obesity within your family, consider it a wake-up call, and start thinking about how you become and live as healthy and healthfully as possible.

MEDICAL CAUSES FOR OBESITY

People who are obese sometimes blame their conditions on medical problems such as hormonal imbalances or slow metabolism. The

An interesting study on how environment affects weight has been conducted for more than 35 years among the Pima Indians in Arizona. The Pimas experience an extremely high obesity rate, and more than half of all adults have diabetes, according to researchers from the National Institutes of Health (NIH). The thing is, a group of Pima Indians living in Sierra Madre, Mexico, has no similar problem with obesity or diabetes, even though they share a very similar genetic makeup with the Pimas in Arizona.

Researchers believe that while living in the desert where food was not always plentiful, the Pimas, over generations, developed or selected these genes that enabled them to store fat. When the lifestyle of the Pima Indians in Arizona became more like that of mainstream America's—meaning that they were involved in much less physical activity and had access to much more calorie-dense food—that ability to store fat became unnecessary and began to work against them. Their Mexican counterparts, however, continued to live a more traditional lifestyle, which incurred long hours of physical activity and a diet high in fiber and starch but low in fat.

As a result, the Pima Indians living in Arizona developed very high rates of obesity and diseases associated with obesity, while the Pima Indians in Mexico did not. Even though both groups are genetically predisposed to obesity, the population that maintained its traditional lifestyle and diet did not become obese. We are not suggesting that everyone should return to a "traditional lifestyle," since a modern lifestyle has many advantages. But these observations in Pimas suggest that, while genetics is a factor, it is not solely responsible for obesity, but rather that obesity is the result of an interaction between a genetic predisposition and an environment conducive to the condition.

If you want to read more about the Pima Indians and how they've worked with NIH researchers to understand, treat, and prevent obesity and diabetes, check out this site: diabetes.niddk.nih.gov/dm/pubs/pima/index.htm.

truth is that hardly anyone who is obese is so because of a medical problem. The very few medical conditions that can result in obesity are usually relatively easy for doctors to identify, meaning that it is almost never necessary to run tests or perform other procedures in an effort to determine why someone is obese.

In rare instances, a condition called *hypothyroidism* can cause obesity. With hypothyroidism, also known as underactive thyroid disease, the thyroid doesn't produce enough hormones, which upsets the balance of chemical reactions within the body. This can result in health problems such as heart disease, infertility, joint pain, and obesity. Children suffering from hypothyroidism usually experience many health issues and are shorter than expected for their age and the height of their parents, whereas most children who are obese tend to be tall for their age because they mature early.

Another rare condition that can result in obesity is *Cushing's syndrome,* which is caused by prolonged exposure to high levels of cortisol, a hormone manufactured within the body by the adrenal glands. People most often develop Cushing's while taking high doses of corticosteroids, which contain a cortisol-like substance.

You may have heard of *leptin deficiency,* which can also cause obesity, but it is an extremely rare condition that has been identified in only a handful of families. *Leptin* is a protein hormone produced by the fat tissue in your body and is necessary for regulating energy balance. Mammals who don't produce enough leptin can eat tremendous amounts of food and still feel hungry, leading to severe obesity.

Some medicines prescribed for various medical conditions, including epilepsy and depression, can also cause excessive weight gain and contribute to obesity. Some of the treatments for cancer can also lead to excessive weight gain and contribute to obesity. On rare occasions, surgery to remove a brain tumor can affect the area of the brain that controls appetite and result in obesity.

If your doctor has prescribed one of those medications mentioned above, or any medication, do not stop taking it because you fear it has caused or might cause you to gain weight. Medicines often are necessary, and if your doctor prescribed it for you, it is because its benefits are greater for you than the risk of gaining weight.

As you've read, however, the disorders that cause obesity are very rare, and responsible for virtually none of the obesity that has become such a concern within our society. Most cases of obesity are what doctors call *common obesity,* and are not caused by medical reasons.

BEHAVIORAL FACTORS THAT CAN CONTRIBUTE TO OBESITY

People eat for many different reasons, not always just because they're hungry. Some people eat when they're stressed out about something, or bored, or sad, or angry. Often, we seek *comfort foods,* foods that make us feel good, and often those foods are calorie dense with little nutritional value. Other people will celebrate with food when they feel happy. This sort of emotional eating not only can get in the way of dealing with whatever is causing a person to be sad or angry; it can also pack on pounds.

Do you ever hear yourself saying something like, "Oh my gosh, I can't believe I ate that whole bowl of potato chips," or "Wow, what happened to all that candy?" If so, you've engaged in what some people call "mindless eating"—a very common practice that has gained attention recently thanks to the research of Dr. Brian Wansink, a former professor of marketing and nutritional science at Cornell University.

Wansink, who has written a book called *Mindless Eating: Why We Eat More than We Think* (Bantam, 2006), claims that the average person makes about 200 food-related decisions every day. Most of those decisions, he says, are made with very little awareness, and most have very little to do with hunger.

His research shows that what people eat is influenced by who is with them, the time of day, how big a plate or bowl they use, where they're eating, and many other factors. Even people who believe they carefully consider everything they eat before consuming it usually are surprised to learn that they eat more than they realize.

Wansink conducted an exercise he called the "bottomless soup bowl study," in which he and other researchers fashioned soup bowls that slowly refilled as people were eating. Paired with other participants who had regular bowls, those with the "bottomless" bowls ate 73 percent more soup, but felt no more full than their peers with regular bowls. The lesson, according to Wansink, is that we judge what we eat with our eyes—not our stomachs. You can read a copy of Wansink's soup study report, learn more about his research, and order his book from his Web site at www.mindlesseating.org.

Realizing that your eating habits are influenced by factors such as where you are and who you're with can actually help you gain control over what you eat. If you know that you eat more than you should when you go to see a movie because you and your friend always share the biggest container of popcorn, break tradition and get the smallest container, and eat it one kernel at a time.

If you eat a package of cupcakes every day when you get home from school because you've always eaten a package of cupcakes at that time, try waiting until dinner to eat, or have fruit or sliced vegetables handy to eat when you come in. We tend to eat what's ready and accessible, so having healthy foods readily available will increase the chances that you'll eat them.

ARE OBESITY AND EATING DISORDERS RELATED?

Questions have been raised as to whether overeating is an eating disorder, and if addressing the issues of overeating and obesity can actually result in eating disorders. *The Diagnostic and Statistical Manual of Mental Disorders,* fourth edition, which is published by the American Psychiatric Association, addresses all known mental health disorders and is relied upon for decisions concerning treatment, insurance coverage, and other issues. The manual lists criteria for three eating disorders: anorexia nervosa, bulimia, and eating disorder not otherwise specified, or EDNOS, which includes eating disorders that don't meet all the criteria necessary to quality as anorexia or bulimia but share some of their characteristics.

Overeating is not considered to be an eating disorder, nor is it considered to be the only reason for obesity. On the other hand, there is concern among many people that efforts to lose weight can result in eating disorders.

As the first symptom of an eating disorder is often dieting, it may appear as if the dieting has "caused" the eating disorder. But eating disorders are complex psychiatric disorders, and are often established before the actual dieting begins. There is conclusive evidence, in fact, that addressing obesity through a medically supervised program does not lead to eating disorders, and may even lessen the likelihood of an eating disorder occurring.

While eating disorders are very unlikely to result from weight loss efforts, you should discuss any concerns you might have with your doctor, parent, school nurse, or another trusted adult.

NO EASY ANSWERS

If you've learned anything from reading this chapter, it probably is that there are no easy answers when it comes to figuring out why people become obese. Obesity is a complex issue that is the subject of much discussion and great debate among the medical community and the general public.

We are, however, learning more about obesity—causes, prevention, and treatments—all the time. It is an important and high-profile health issue, and expectations are high that we will continue to discover more and more about why people become obese.

WHAT YOU NEED TO KNOW

➤ Energy balance occurs when you eat the same amount of energy in the form of calories as you expend in activity, growing, and just staying alive. Energy imbalance occurs when you consume either more or less energy than you expend.

➤ Biological and genetic factors can increase a person's risk of becoming overweight or obese, as can some medical conditions.

➤ While genetic factors might make you predisposed to obesity, there are lifestyle choices you can make to minimize the risk.

➤ Some habits and behaviors also can contribute to a person's chances of becoming obese.

➤ Scientists and doctors are learning more all the time about obesity and its causes, but many questions still remain.

3

How Our Environments Work Against Us

Kareen lives in a neighborhood of row homes and apartment buildings, with a few corner stores, a fast-food restaurant, and a church nearby. A 10th grader, she walks the half-mile or so back and forth to school every day, but that's about the only exercise she gets since there's no more gym class and kids her age don't have outside recess.

Her mom has two jobs and works until seven or eight P.M., and, because Kareen is the oldest of five children, she's responsible for coming home after school to keep an eye on her brothers and sisters. Sometimes she and her friend stop on the way home for a soda or a snack, but after that, she's pretty much stuck in the house with the kids.

It's Kareen's job to get dinner ready for her siblings. Her brothers and sisters like macaroni and cheese, and she often will heat up canned pasta or add hot water to packaged noodles to make soup. Sometimes Kareen's mom stops on her way home from work and gets them cheeseburgers and fries from the restaurant up the block, and she tries to keep snack foods in the house for the kids to eat when they come home hungry from school.

Kareen knows that she's overweight, and most of her brothers and sisters are, too. She'd like to take the kids to the playground around the corner, but her mom says it's not safe because drug dealers hang out there. She's thought about asking her mom if she can join a gym, but there's not money for things like that and besides, how would she get there?

23

Kareen often feels stuck, and sometimes gets resentful and sad about having to care for her brothers and sisters. She doesn't have many friends because she can't go anyplace, so she pretty much watches TV. At least there usually are cookies. Those make her feel a little better.

While there are many questions concerning the causes of obesity and explanations for the pronounced increase in the rate of obesity during the past decades, it is generally agreed that the environments in which we live play a significant role. Most of us live in environments that work against our ability to achieve and maintain healthy weights. These have been called *obesogenic environments,* or environments that generate obesity. In short, our environments actually encourage us to be sedentary and to consume more calories than needed.

While daily life for most people used to involve some walking, many people today don't need to walk more than a few steps at any given time. We have garage-door openers; remote controls for TVs, fans, and lights; electric washers, dryers, mixers, and vacuum cleaners; and many other appliances to make our work easier. No longer do we have to scrub laundry by hand, hang rugs over wash lines and beat them to clean them, or even get out of cars to open our garages. Technology has significantly reduced the need for us to expend energy, but at the same time, we keep getting the message from advertisers to buy and eat more food.

While you know that you'd benefit from walking that mile to school rather than hitching a ride from Dad every day, it may be that there are no sidewalks along the busy road that leads to the school and it would be dangerous for you to walk. Maybe, you'd love to grab some fresh fruit on the way home, but the only store you pass is a convenience store where the closest thing to a fruit is the blue raspberry soda or a fruit-filled Danish. Our environments sometimes make it very difficult—even impossible—to make good choices concerning food and physical activity. While we're told that we need to take personal responsibility for how we eat and live, our environments sometimes don't allow us to claim that responsibility, or may at least make it very difficult.

The role of the environment in obesity is complex and multifaceted, and involves our homes, schools, and communities. Environmental factors also include advertising and marketing of foods, education about nutrition and exercise, and resources available to different groups of people.

In this chapter, we'll take a look at how our environments work against us when it comes to controlling weight. You'll begin to understand that our environments actually encourage us to be inactive, and how lessening that inactivity can have far-reaching and positive consequences. By recognizing those outside influences, you'll begin to develop the tools you need to make your own decisions and to gain autonomy from the external forces that influence the choices you make.

As we discussed in chapter 2, energy balance has two components: calories consumed and calories expended. You read that you burn off calories just by being, as well as for growth or when you move around during physical activity. The calories you consume, of course, come from the foods and beverages that you eat and drink. Where you live—your house, neighborhood, community, and school—influences both sides of the energy equation: what you consume and what you expend.

YOUR HOME AND FAMILY

Your home environment probably has a lot to do with your energy balance, or energy imbalance. That's because it most likely is the place where you do most of your eating and where you spend much of your free time. Let's first consider your house, and how what's in it affects your energy output.

Opportunities to engage in *sedentary activity* have increased dramatically during the past 20 or 30 years, and kids, teens, and adults

In addition to soda, there is a quickly growing market of sweetened beverages–including sports drinks, teas, and vitamin-enhanced waters and juices–many of which can add calories quickly. A popular sports drink, for instance, contains 50 calories per eight ounces, but typically is sold in 20- or 32-ounce bottles, so one bottle contains 125 to 200 calories. The same goes for a popular iced tea. An eight-ounce *serving* contains 100 calories, but it's sold in 20-ounce bottles, increasing the chances that the consumer will drink more than one serving. Manufacturers and markers would have you believe that you can't live without these "enhanced" beverages, but the reality is they provide unnecessary calories and don't offer significant nutritional value to a balanced diet.

are embracing those opportunities. Computer games are fun. Video games are even more fun. You've got to check Facebook every day, and nobody wants to be the only kid in school who didn't see the latest episode of *Lost*. Unfortunately, hanging out on the computer or watching TV doesn't call for much physical exertion, and results in minimal energy expenditure.

In addition, it's possible that your home simply doesn't offer opportunity for physical activity. Maybe you don't have a yard where you can toss a football or jump rope, or space for a basketball hoop or gym equipment. It often seems like the cards are stacked against us in favor of inactivity, even when we want to be physically active.

Take a minute or two to assess opportunities for physical activity within your home, and to look at factors that may discourage activity. Does your family own a treadmill or exercise bike? Does your house have stairs you need to go up and down frequently? Are there TVs in every bedroom that encourage extra viewing? You might be surprised to realize how your home environment affects your energy expenditure.

The other half of the energy balance, what we eat and drink, also has changed during the last couple of decades, including at home. Many families rely more on take-out foods or quick-to-make frozen or packaged foods than they used to. An ever-increasing variety of snack foods, many of them high in fat and calories, is available. And researchers at the University of North Carolina at Chapel Hill reported that between 1977 and 2001, our energy intake from sweetened beverages, like soda and fruit juice, increased 135 percent, while energy intake from milk decreased by 38 percent. Overall, we consume 278 more calories a day on average from the beverages we drink than we did 30 years ago, due not only to what we drink, but to portion size and frequency of our consumption of sweetened beverages.

This shift in eating habits isn't overly surprising when you consider that more than twice as many moms work outside the home today as they did in 1970, leaving less time to prepare, serve, and eat meals at home. Nearly three-quarters of all women between the ages of 25 to 56 work, according to the Pew Research Center, a nonprofit organization that provides information about trends affecting America. This puts a time squeeze on both one-parent and two-parent families, forcing them to take shortcuts that aren't always in the best interests of health when it comes to meals.

Do a little food exploring in your house. What do you see when you first open the refrigerator door? That's important, because researchers say we often eat the first thing that we see. In a perfect world you'd see ready-to-eat fruits and vegetables instead of calorie-dense snack foods. Is there a jar of cookies on your counter? Potato chips in the snack drawer? If so, the availability of these foods is likely to be tempting you to consume extra calories.

If other members of your household don't get healthy food and exercise, it can be even more difficult for you to do so. Families tend to engage in similar behaviors, and it's quite likely that your parents have passed along more to you than their genes. Ever since

Scott worries about his weight a lot, especially when kids at school tease him and laugh at him during gym class because he can't keep up.

Sometimes Scott thinks about going out for a sport at school, but he's afraid to try because other kids might make fun of him. Besides, he's got music lessons twice a week and rehearsals on Saturday, so he probably wouldn't have time.

An 11th grader, Scott lives in a housing development in the suburbs, miles away from school. His dad drops him off every day on his way to work because it's easier than waiting for the bus, and you can't ride a bike or walk because there are no sidewalks along the roads you have to take. He usually gets a ride home with Justin, a kid who lives in his neighborhood. If he has a music lesson his mom might pick him up and drive him there.

He and Justin almost always stop at a fast-food place on their way home for a snack, and have made sort of a hobby of finding the best deals. They've pretty much tried everything on the dollar menus of every restaurant. They're always hungry by then because the school lunches are really bad and they often end up just eating a couple of bags of chips and some cookies along with some iced tea or something.

Scott likes a little downtime when he gets home, so he usually plays video games or gets on Facebook for a while before he starts his home-work. Sometimes his dad stops on his way home from work and picks up dinner from a restaurant with curbside service. That makes it easier for his mom, who often has meetings at night or has to finish work in her home office.

Scott thinks things might be better for him once he gets his license and can drive himself. That way he won't always be waiting for a ride, and he'll be able to go when and where he wants to.

you were little, you've learned from their example, whether you realized it or not.

Our homes and families have changed along with society at large, resulting in a lot of positive changes and improvements in the quality of life, but also in some challenges—sometimes at the price of our health.

YOUR NEIGHBORHOOD

The neighborhoods in which many of us live also contribute to an obesogenic environment. Maybe you're fortunate enough to live in a neighborhood where there are sidewalks on which you can walk to school, or streets that are safe to bike along. Maybe crime is not an issue where you live, and you even have a park with tennis courts just down the street from you. If so, you're fortunate.

In many communities, it's nearly impossible to walk or ride a bike in safety because there are no sidewalks or crosswalks, and roadways are divided by concrete barriers. And high levels of crime make some areas unsafe and force residents to pretty much remain indoors.

Limited recreation space also is a factor in how our neighborhoods may contribute to an increase in the obesity rate. Many areas don't include accessible and well-maintained recreational space or facilities like playgrounds, ball fields, and parks, making it difficult to find a place to engage in physical activity.

Studies have revealed that, in some areas, a lack of supermarkets forces residents to shop at smaller stores where fresh, healthy foods are not as plentiful, and, when available, often cost more than they would in large supermarkets. One study concluded that children who live in areas where fruit and vegetables are readily available and affordable have significantly less weight gain between kindergarten and third grade than children who live in areas where those items are less readily available, or where there's a prevalence of fast-food restaurants.

Think about your neighborhood and whether it contributes to obesity. If there's a grocery or convenience store nearby, what kinds of foods can you buy there? Are your choices limited to high-calorie snack foods, or is there opportunity to buy fruit, low-fat yogurt, and other healthy snacks? What sort of restaurants are in your neighborhood? What food-related advertising do you see near your home or school? What advertisements are on the billboards around your house or school? Do they promote physical activity or TV shows? Conduct a little survey to help you think about how your environment might be affecting your weight and your health.

The good news is that many of the problems discussed above have been identified, and much attention is being given to them. Since 2003, the U.S. Department of Health and Human Services has partnered with more than 50 cities to improve public health by addressing health-related problems and issues within the city's communities, schools, and workplaces. Researchers have teamed up with local and city governments and planners to implement more user-friendly environments in areas where nonmotorized transportation is currently difficult or impossible.

Until these important changes have taken place, which may take years, you're pretty much on your own. Becoming conscious of your environment and how it affects you is the first step in learning how to navigate it so that your choices are not dictated by the outside, but rather by your own independent and conscious decisions.

YOUR SCHOOL

Once you get to school, chances are that you'll spend much of the day sitting—not engaging in physical activity. Most schools offer some sort of activity, but in many cases, gym classes or other opportunities to move around have been shortened due to academic pressures or lack of resources, including facilities, staff, and funding. Many adults also spend most of their workday sitting.

While you probably aren't getting a lot of exercise during the school day, you may be getting the opportunity to eat a lot of foods that can result in weight gain. While efforts are made to improve the healthiness of the federally reimbursable meals schools offer, many schools have added food options, known as "competitive foods," that may tempt students to eat unhealthy foods or consume more than they need.

Your school might have vending machines in various locations from which you can buy high-calorie candy or baked goods that often contain trans fats, which are known to raise *cholesterol* levels and increase the risk of heart disease. Sweetened drinks also are available for sale in vending machines in some schools, while water may not be. Some schools sell snacks in bookstores or other handy spots, and many offer à la carte items in their cafeterias, including sweetened drinks and snack items. Some schools even bring in restaurant chains to sell pizzas or other foods on particular days.

National attention has been directed toward this issue, largely because of a report issued in 2007 by the Institute of Medicine calling for competitive foods to comply with federal dietary guidelines in order for them to be permitted in schools. The report also called for schools to make plain, unflavored water available for free throughout the day to students, and to limit other available beverages. While many schools have addressed or are addressing these issues, there is still work to be done in improving the nutritional value of available foods.

Schools also contribute to our country's obesity problem in other ways. Many schools allow soda companies or fast-food chains to promote their products in exchange for cash or other incentives. A soda manufacturer, for example, might pay for all school athletic uniforms if the school agrees to sell only that manufacturer's products in its vending machines and at sporting events and other activities. Many schools depend on this cash to sustain programs. The reason soda and other companies do this is that they know that most people are loyal to the brand they chose during adolescence. When a company convinces an adolescent to choose its brand, it wins a client for life! So companies will do everything to capture your loyalty to their brands at your age.

Consider where else food pops up in schools. Kids are urged to sell candy, cookie dough, and pizzas for fund-raisers. In younger grades, birthdays are celebrated with cupcakes or other treats, and some teachers still use candy or other foods to reward their students.

While none of those practices is necessarily a problem on its own, when you consider that you spend a majority of your waking hours in school, and many students stay for after-school activities, having calorie-dense foods available throughout the day in a variety of circumstances clearly can contribute to consuming more calories than is necessary to achieve energy balance.

GETTING AROUND

Americans love their cars. Over time we've become increasingly dependent on the automobile, with many people driving distances they easily could walk or bike. That's not to say that cars aren't useful and necessary for many people. Sprawling communities make it difficult or impossible for many people to get to school, work, shopping, and other activities without a motor vehicle. It's pretty rare for people who live outside of cities to be able to walk to the grocery store, doctor, bank, and other necessary destinations. Sometimes it's not so much a matter of distance from home to other locations but a matter of practicality. Some areas are difficult to traverse because streets don't connect with one another, or culs-de-sac empty out onto high-volume highways. And public transportation in those same areas is often inadequate or nonexistent, meaning that the only way to get from one place to another is to drive or, in the case of many adolescents, to get a ride from parents or friends.

You probably won't be surprised to hear that the amount of time spent driving or riding in a car has been linked to the likelihood of obesity. A study of 11,000 residents of the Atlanta, Georgia, area showed that every 30 minutes of time spent in a car each day increased the likelihood of obesity by 3 percent.

People who live in cities often rely on public transportation, although many city dwellers also have cars. In short, cars and other motorized transportation are the primary methods of getting around for most Americans. While easy and convenient, these do not aid in efforts to stem the increasing rate of obesity.

Once you get to where you're going, it often doesn't get any better. In many buildings, people are directed into elevators rather than to steps. Even when you really want to do the right thing and take the stairs to go up two floors, it may be difficult or impossible to find the stairs. Often, the way our environment is built not only limits our freedom to make the better choice, but it usually encourages you, consciously or unconsciously, to make the wrong choice. Some businesses and institutions offer shuttle services rather than having visitors walk from a distant parking area or traverse a large campus. Students ride buses or public transportation to school because it's too far, too hazardous, or too difficult to walk. All of these factors contribute to decreased activity and increased risk for obesity.

WHAT, AND HOW MUCH, YOU EAT

Life has changed, and so has what we eat and how we eat. A generation ago, three-quarters of the average American family's food budget was spent on foods that were prepared and eaten at home. Today, about half of that family's food money is spent eating outside the home. Restaurant portions have increased dramatically, and not only at fast-food establishments. Researchers at Pennsylvania State University and Clemson University in South Carolina polled chefs from restaurants including upscale, cafeteria, and casual eateries, and found that more than half of them were piling up portions up to three times the recommended size for meat, and four times for pasta.

Consider, for example, that when fast-food restaurants became popular during the 1950s, a soda was served in a seven-ounce cup and the supersized burger of that day was made with a little more than three ounces of meat divided into two patties. Today, a child-size soda is 12 ounces, and a large is 32 ounces—an entire quart. Convenience-store shoppers can buy giant 64-ounce containers of

The average daily caloric needs for an adolescent female are 1,800 calories, and an adolescent male, 2,200. Now consider a typical "combo meal" at a fast-food restaurant near you. Let's say you decide to order a crispy chicken sandwich that comes with medium fries and a medium drink. At one popular fast-food place, the calories add up like this: 550 for the sandwich, plus 70 more for a package of honey-mustard sauce; 380 for the fries, plus 30 more for a couple of packs of ketchup; and 210 for a medium soda. That comes to a grand total of 1,240 calories—well over half of the daily recommended amount for either a female or male.

soda marketed as single servings. The supersized burger at one fast food restaurant today contains an astounding 12.6 ounces of beef and more than 900 calories—four times the amount of the 1950s version. Even a regular hamburger now contains more meat than that first super-sized sandwich.

It can be very tricky to know how many calories you're actually consuming, or which foods are better for you. Some people will order a chicken or fish sandwich instead of a burger, thinking that it's healthier. Or they'll get a salad from a fast-food restaurant, thinking they're actually making a healthy choice. Consider these facts however, which are obtained from one fast-food restaurant's own nutrition facts for popular menu items.

➤ A quarter-pound burger with cheese contains 510 calories, while a crispy chicken club sandwich contains 660 calories.
➤ A Caesar salad with chicken sounds like a good nutritional value with 220 calories. If the chicken is crispy (fried) instead of grilled, you'll need to add 130 calories. If you use a package of dressing and a package of croutons, however, you'll need to add another 250 calories, and now your salad no longer sounds quite so healthy. In fact, with the crispy chicken, croutons, and dressing, that salad would contain as many calories as two regular hamburgers.
➤ A large order of fries contains more than twice as many calories as a small order (570 compared to 250).

> ➤ A five-piece serving of chicken breast strips contains 670 calories, and if you choose the creamy ranch dressing for dipping, you'll add another 200 calories.
> ➤ A triple-thick chocolate shake comes in four sizes, ranging from 12 to 32 ounces, and from 440 to 1,660 calories. Pair up just the smallest shake with those chicken breast strips mentioned above and you're up to half or more of your daily caloric requirement. The largest size shake alone will give you nearly all of your calories requirements for the day!

It's difficult to make good choices at restaurants, especially fast food restaurants, because nutritional information often isn't easily accessible, or may be accessible only on the wrappings once you've purchased the food. Many fast food restaurants now provide nutrition information, including the number of calories for each food choice, but you might have to work hard to find it. Some cities have started to mandate that chain restaurants post the number of calories next to the price on menus, giving customers concerned with making healthier choices easy access to the information they need before purchasing their food.

The restaurant industry and marketers are hard at work getting us to eat more. One national chain restaurant claimed in 2007 to be the "first casual dining chain to offer smaller portions at lower prices all day." Smaller portions sounds good, right? That same restaurant, however, suggests on its menu that diners who exercised restraint by ordering a smaller-portion meal are likely to have room left over for dessert.

Increased availability of processed supermarket convenience foods also has changed the way we eat. It might be fast and convenient to brown a pound of ground meat and add it to a packaged mix that, with very little work, results in a cheesy pasta dish. One cup of that mixture, though, can contain nearly 400 calories and hefty portions of fat and salt. Frozen pizzas topped with pepperoni and sausage might be tasty, but not the most nutritionally sound choices.

WHAT YOU WATCH

Television is a pervasive and important presence in American culture, serving as a primary source of information and entertainment for millions of Americans. While TV watching can be educational and informative, excessive TV viewing is associated with increased risk of obesity for several reasons. First, most people don't move around much while they watch television. Sure, you could do jumping jacks or jog in place or walk on a treadmill while you watch, but most people

It's difficult to pin down exactly how much TV kids and teens are watching, but a nationwide survey in 2007 (Youth Risk Behavior Surveillance) found that more than 35 percent of high school students reported watching TV for a minimum of three hours on an average school day.

sit or lie down to watch TV. So most people don't expend many calories as they catch up on the latest *Grey's Anatomy*. A second factor is that watching TV and snacking seem to go together, and many people consume a lot of extra calories while watching their favorite shows. This increased calorie consumption is encouraged, of course, by all the commercials you see while you're watching TV. How many times have you gotten the message that a football game isn't a football game without pizza, salty snacks, and your favorite soda, or that your favorite fast food restaurant is offering a limited-time-only special sandwich, and will be open late tonight for your convenience? And sitting for long periods of time may reduce resting metabolism, meaning that the rate at which your body burns calories is slowed.

So, you ask, how much TV is too much TV? It is the recommendation of the American Academy of Pediatrics that kids and teens spend no more than two hours a day watching TV or engaging in other sedentary activities, such as playing electronic games, Internet chatting or surfing, or text messaging. Time spent on the computer for homework, however, is not included in this other "screen time."

Limiting your TV viewing not only increases the chances that you'll be engaging in more activities that require greater energy expenditure, but also decreases exposure to advertising and the temptation to snack. Lots of teenagers claim they're not influenced by television commercials, but it's a sure bet that advertisers wouldn't spend millions of dollars to promote their products if the commercials didn't influence us.

KEEP ON EATING, BABY!

The food and beverage industry spends billions of dollars for advertising every year, making the message clear that we are to eat, eat,

eat. Its efforts have paid off. Research has shown that advertising influences the foods we like and buy. And most foods advertised are high in calories and low in nutrients. Food and beverage advertisements are nearly impossible to miss, as they show up in abundance on TV, the Internet, billboards, and in magazines and newspapers. It's reported that in 2004 the food industry spent $11 billion on advertising, and that $5 billion of that was in TV ads.

Not all of us see the same ads, however, because different groups of consumers are exposed to different advertisements. Ads designed to appeal to kids, for instance, will employ cartoon characters to promote a product, while ads for similar products that are designed to appeal to teens might use entertainers or athletes.

African-American and Latino audiences, which tend to have higher prevalence of obesity than white audiences, are exposed to more ads for high-calorie, low-nutrient foods than white audiences, both on TV and in magazines. A child who watches five hours of television will spend a full hour watching commercials, with about half of them advertising food. And food and beverage marketers have recently come up with some nontraditional and creative means of targeting teens, often without the knowledge of their parents.

Marketers have gone digital in their efforts to reach teens, according to a May 2007 report from the Berkeley Media Studies Group and the Center for Digital Democracy, a nonprofit organization that monitors digital communications in an effort to assure they remain in the best interests of the public. The report included the following examples of digital advertising, specifically intended to reach adolescents and teens:

> ➤ In California, 600 fast-food restaurants joined in a campaign urging cell-phone users to text a special phone number in order to receive an instant electronic coupon for a frozen dessert.
> ➤ A fast-food chain posted videos promoting their products on YouTube. A video promoting the chain's junior menu, in which a young girl is showed buying a burger and shake on her own for the first time, was viewed more than 300,000 times.
> ➤ A major candy company contracted with a popular teen music group to make "webisodes" promoting its product.

Many teens deny that marketing affects their buying decisions, but the truth is that it does. And a lot of marketing is done in a way that you don't even notice, such as having certain products appear within the content of a show instead of during a commercial. This is called *brand placement,* and companies spend a lot of money to have their products show up during your favorite shows and movies. It's not just by chance or her own choice that your favorite actress grabs a particular type of soda or other beverage rather than a glass of tap water. You may not notice it during the movie, but next time you're in the store, you may choose that same beverage because unconsciously you associate it with the actress you like or how much fun you had watching her movie. Next time you watch a movie or a TV show, try to pay attention to how often brand placement occurs. Brand placement now even happens within video games. If you don't think these advertisements influence you, make a note of all the products you buy in the coming week, and then consider which of those products you've seen ads or brand placements for, and how many you've never seen advertised. This will help you to realize that most of the time you don't choose a product that you've never seen advertised or placed in a TV show, a movie, or at one of your school's sporting events. Nearly everyone with access to media is influenced by marketing and advertising, including you.

While your environment can work against you, understanding the factors that contribute to inactivity and obesity can empower you to make better choices and can increase your awareness of your situation.

WHAT YOU NEED TO KNOW

> Most of us live in obesogenic environments, or environments that generate obesity. These environments work against our ability to achieve and maintain healthy weights.

> Your home environment could also promote obesity, both by what is available for you to eat there and what is available for your leisure time there.

> Neighborhoods that aren't conducive to walking, cycling, and other physical activities also are risk factors for obesity, as are schools that offer high-calorie foods and minimal physical activity.

> Doctors recommend that teens engage in no more than two hours of TV viewing or other screen time a day.

> Large portion sizes, large dishes, increased availability of food, food marketing, and other factors are prevalent in society, and all contribute to overeating and obesity.

Fighting Back against the Obesogenic Environment

While it's true that our environments work against us in our efforts to achieve and maintain a healthy weight, it's also true that knowledge is power, and once you understand the challenges you face, you can begin to overcome them or work around them and start making healthy changes possible. In fact, working for these changes in your environment may make you a leader in advocating for changes that would positively affect not only you, but your friends, family members, schoolmates, and community members.

The good news is that there is extensive and ongoing research into how our environments can be improved in order to promote healthy weight. A comprehensive set of recommendations has been offered in a report compiled by the Institute of Medicine (IOM), a nongovernmental, not-for-profit agency that was formed in 1970 with the purpose of providing advice to the nation on important topics such as health, medical science, and medicine.

The Institute of Medicine in 2004 released a report called *Preventing Childhood Obesity: Health in the Balance,* which addressed the issue of obesity among children and youth and provided recommendations for how schools, communities, and families can work to prevent obesity and encourage good health.

In this chapter, you'll learn about some of those recommendations, as well as other suggestions on how you might be able to help implement some changes in your home, school, and community.

AT HOME

As you read in chapter 3, your home and family environments are significant factors affecting energy balance. If your family is always on the go, gets lots of exercise, and most often eats foods that are low in calories and high in healthy nutrients, chances are that you share those traits. If your family mostly enjoys sedentary activities like watching TV and playing computer games and most often eats foods that are dense in calories, it's likely that you share these habits with them.

   If you're concerned that your family's lifestyle isn't as healthy as it could be, you can be an advocate for change. You can make some changes that can help to improve your health and the health of your family. Start with the changes in areas over which you have control, such as your own bedroom. It will show to your family that you are serious about this, and, following your example, family members may be more likely to help you implement changes in areas of the house that you don't directly control. This is especially important if you have brothers and sisters—particularly if they're younger than you—because you can help them decrease their risk of obesity in the future. So, let's take a few minutes to think about some changes you can make—or at least talk to a parent about making.

> ► If you have a TV in your room, move it out today. If you own it, sell it to a thrift shop, and use the money to buy a good *pedometer* to monitor the number of steps you take each day, or to have the bicycle that's rusting in the garage fixed. Studies have shown that kids and teens with TVs in their bedrooms weigh more than those without TVs. The easier and more convenient TV viewing is, the more you're likely to watch instead of participating in less sedentary activities.
>
> ► Stop eating in your room. Changing just that one habit is easy, but important. Make an effort to only eat sitting at a table, with the TV off, and from a small plate. Decide consciously when serving your food how much you really need to eat, and stop eating when you've finished that portion.
>
> ► Ask for healthier food choices. If the kitchen counter, the refrigerator, and the cabinets are filled with high-calorie foods that aren't good for you, ask the person who does the shopping for your home to substitute more healthy choices. Better still, go along to the store on family shopping trips and check labels before putting items in your cart to assure you're getting foods that are nutritious and are lower in calories, fat, and sugar.

➤ Get involved with your food preparation in your home. Offer to help peel and cut up vegetables, and make low-fat dips with fat-free yogurt or fat-free sour cream. Monitor how much cream, butter, and cheese is used in your family's favorite recipes. Volunteer to help prepare healthy meals. Who knows? You might find that you love to cook!

➤ Encourage your family to sit at the table and eat together. Studies have indicated that family members of all ages tend to eat more grains, fruits, vegetables, and other healthy foods, and fewer unhealthy foods, when eating together. And whatever you do, avoid the temptation to watch TV while you eat. Research has indicated that TV viewing during dinner results in greater intake of red meat, salty foods, soda, and pizza.

➤ Eat at home as often as possible, avoiding delivery and take-out foods. Sure, everybody likes to go out to lunch or dinner on occasion, but a steady diet of restaurants, particularly fast-food restaurants, can negatively affect your energy balance and your health.

➤ Find a place in or outside of your house where you can exercise. Maybe your family doesn't own any exercise equipment, but you can still engage in physical activity by jogging in place, climbing steps, working out to an aerobics DVD, or jumping rope. The important thing is that you get some sort of physical activity, not how or where you get it.

Sure, there are factors in your home that you won't be able to change. You can't pick up your house or apartment building and move it to spot that would be more conducive to outdoor activities, and other family members would probably scream in protest if you suggested getting rid of all the televisions in the house. Still, you can encourage others in your home to read this book, or share the information that you've read in order to better educate your entire family about creating an environment that makes healthy choices not only possible, but easy to achieve. It's less difficult to make changes when everyone is in agreement and working together. If getting rid of all the televisions in the house is too much for your family to cope with, try one little step by negotiating a "no TV or electronic games" week a few times a year. They will see that one actually can survive for a week without TV! Call it "Survivor Screen-Free Island" and see who will be voted off the island first. You'll be surprised about all the other things you can do, together or individually during these weeks with all the time you have because you're not watching TV!

AT SCHOOL

Schools are strongly encouraged to become partners in the nation's obesity prevention efforts, and, if you're willing, you could serve as a voice at your school to raise awareness of those efforts. You are not powerless. If you make your voice heard, you very well may discover there are people within your school who want to help you. As increasing attention is being given to obesity among kids and teens, schools are being encouraged to play important roles in addressing the problem. You might be able to help jump-start your school's efforts by taking action as suggested below.

> ▸ Increase your awareness of your school environment by learning about the factors that influence it. You can learn about what constitutes a healthy school environment by accessing the Centers for Disease Control and Prevention School Health Index. The index addresses physical activity, healthy eating, tobacco use, safety, and asthma, and was designed to enable schools to assess their environments and make changes that will benefit the health of students. You can access the School Health Index at apps.nccd.cdc.gov/shi/default.aspx.
> ▸ Once you're familiar with issues that affect the health of your school environment, you can talk to your school nurse, or a teacher or administrator, about initiating a project to assess

A two-year study involving 10 schools in Philadelphia revealed that making even little changes within participating schools resulted in cutting the number of kids who become overweight during that period by 50 percent compared to kids in the non participating schools. Five schools implemented better nutritional policies, teacher and student education, outreach to families to participate in healthier eating, and rewards for kids who ate healthy snacks or avoided snacks. In the schools where interventions were made, only 7.5 percent of students became overweight, compared to 15 percent in the five schools that served as comparisons. The study tells us that changing school environments has a huge impact on the health of students.

School districts across the country and abroad are taking note of a program called the Walking School Bus, which is simply a group of kids accompanied by at least one adult who walk along a particular route to school, picking up other kids along the way, so that kids can walk to school safely instead of having to ride the bus. If you're interested in implementing a Walking School Bus for the younger kids in your school district, you can learn more at www.walkingschoolbus.org.

your school environment and identify changes that could be made to improve that environment. If your school requires a project in order to graduate, you could volunteer to initiate the project yourself, or enlist some friends to help you.

➤ Speak up against fund-raisers that sell cookie dough, pizzas or pizza kits, candy, and other unhealthy foods. Suggest instead that your school sponsor a car wash, or a five-kilometer race on its track, cross-country course, or the local park, or conduct a fund-raiser that doesn't involve food, such as a book sale.

➤ If your school allows soda companies, fast-food restaurants, or other producers of unhealthy foods to sponsor sports programs by providing uniforms or other equipment in exchange for advertising or sales rights on school property, try to find an alternative sponsor to replace them. Perhaps a store that sells electronics or a department store in your community would be glad to pick up a sponsorship. It can't hurt to ask, and you may end up doing you and your schoolmates a favor by eliminating the advertisement and sale of unhealthy foods at your school.

➤ Offer to help design and assist with implementing health awareness programs for younger children in your school district. Childhood obesity is an increasing concern as well as obesity in teens.

IN YOUR COMMUNITY

Increasing attention is being given to community design and land use, as problems associated with poor planning, such as obesity, become more apparent. In 2000 the CDC launched Healthy Places, a program

Other sources of information about community design for health living include Active Living by Design at www.activelivingbydesign.org, and the Community Tool Box. Active Living by Design looks at how community design affects the activity levels of residents, and comes up with innovative approaches for increasing activity by improving design. The Community Tool Box, designed and operated by the University of Kansas, is a free resource for people who want to acquire the necessary skills to contribute to the building of healthy communities.

designed to promote safe, user-friendly communities. The program address issues such as accessibility, children's health and the *built environment,* health impact assessment, physical activity, and respiratory health and air pollution. You can learn more about Healthy Places and get an idea of how healthy your community is at www. cdc.gov/healthyplaces.

As a teenager, you may not be in a position to establish policy. You can, however, begin learning about what makes a healthy community, and identify changes that may be necessary within your community. Consider the suggestions listed below.

> Educate your friends about your community environment and encourage them to get involved. Teenagers can have a powerful voice when they speak out together for change and improvement that will make them healthier.
> Get involved with local health organizations or a local chapter of a health organization such as the American Heart Association or the American Diabetes Association. Team up with other concerned teens in your school or community to ask representatives of those organizations to consider sponsoring, supporting, or even creating new initiatives to improve your community environment. You may be surprised how important it is for them that the need be identified by teens in the community.
> Team up with local organizations to improve safety in your neighborhood, so that you and everyone else can feel safer playing, walking, or biking in the streets and parks. In some

neighborhoods it may help to volunteer with the local town watch; in other neighborhoods it may be slowing cars down by installing speed bumps.

➤ Most municipalities have recreation boards that oversee parks, playgrounds, biking trails, and so forth. Get in touch with a member of your recreation board and ask if you can talk to someone about community efforts to improve recreational space and opportunities for teens.

➤ Organize a walking club or a tennis group, and get your friends to be active with you. Physical activity is fun when you're having a good time with friends.

You'll read much more in later chapters about making changes to improve your own health. Some of the ideas mentioned here to change your environment will help to get you started by making it easier to choose healthy alternatives.

WHAT YOU NEED TO KNOW

➤ While your environment may work against you, there are steps you can take to minimize the ill effects and maximize opportunities for healthy living.

➤ You may not be able to establish policy yet, but you can be a voice to advocate for changes in your environment at home, in your school, and in your neighborhood.

➤ Team up with teens, adults, and local and national organizations to propose and help implement initiatives that will improve your school and community. If knowledge is power, teamwork is the tool to achieve changes.

➤ Many adults and some of your peers will be impressed with your efforts to make your environment more conducive to good health. Don't be afraid to suggest ideas.

5

How Being Obese Affects You Socially, Psychologically, and Physically

Alex is a 16-year-old boy whose parents moved to California from Mexico before Alex was born. He's a good student and has lots of friends, but lately Alex hasn't been feeling well.

He's been really tired, he seems to always be thirsty, and he's getting up two or three times a night to use the bathroom. His mom is worried that he has a urinary infection, so she makes an appointment at the clinic.

The doctor at the clinic knows Alex and his family's medical background, and he suspects what the problem is right away. Sure enough, a blood test reveals that Alex's blood sugar is extremely high, and he's developed diabetes.

The doctor isn't overly surprised, but Alex and his parents are in shock. Even though Alex's dad and a lot of relatives have diabetes, they never thought Alex would get it at this age. He's a little overweight, but not nearly as obese as other kids in school. He eats about the same foods as the rest of his family and his friends, and he and his friends sometimes throw a football around outside.

And yet now he'll have to take insulin and have blood tests several times a day and be really careful about what he eats. The doctor said Alex had a very high predisposition to diabetes because of his genetic background, but that doesn't make Alex feel any better. He begins to feel depressed and starts to stay inside more, avoiding his friends and looking for excuses not to go out. After a while his friends stop calling him, and he feels worse than ever—angry and bitter about his condition and rejected by his friends. His grades drop dramatically, and

Alex makes excuses to miss school every chance he gets. His parents are extremely worried, even fearing that Alex might do something to hurt himself.

If you are overweight or obese, you probably have already experienced some problems associated with your condition. Perhaps you've had some health-related difficulties, such as breathing problems or high blood pressure. Or, you might have already experienced some psychological or social difficulties associated with being obese.

Unfortunately, obesity is considered by many people to be an undesirable characteristic, resulting in a stigma, or rejection of those who are obese. Adolescents and teenagers can be extremely hard on themselves, and on each other. If you've been bullied or teased as a result of your weight, you know how devastating and hurtful it can be. Many overweight teens end up feeling bad about themselves, hating how they look, and wishing they could look differently.

Studies have concluded that obese teens have a lower health-related quality of life than those who are not obese, and that obesity affects how teens function physically, emotionally, socially, and academically. While this is not good news for obese teens, it's important to remember that there are steps you can take that will make improvements in all of the areas mentioned above.

For instance, you can talk with a guidance counselor or someone else who can help you come up with strategies to use if you're teased about your weight. Studies have shown that obese teens who participate in sports or school clubs tend to have more friends than those who stay at home and watch TV. If your grades have been impacted, you could ask about getting extra help. And there are many changes you can make to improve your physical health, even without having to first lose a large amount of weight.

To begin, let's look at how obese people can be impacted socially, and examine some of the prejudices and biases they encounter.

SOCIAL IMPACTS OF OVERWEIGHT AND OBESITY

Despite its prevalence, obesity is often looked down upon in our society. Being obese makes someone likely to experience discrimination, which can affect what schools or jobs will be available, as well as one's earnings, marital status, and overall quality of life.

This discrimination occurs in adult, teen, and child populations, and can have devastating consequences to a person's emotional and physical health, professional condition, and social situation.

University researchers have developed the Implicit Association Test, which employs a high-speed word-association exercise to discover attitudes toward people who are obese or overweight. Many people don't recognize that they're prejudiced against obese people. In fact, many obese people have the same weight bias against other obese people as the rest of the population. If you share this bias, it's likely that you don't even know it. The test, which takes about 20 minutes to complete, can help you to discover whether you are biased against overweight or obese people. You can access the test on the Internet at implicit.harvard.edu/implicit. Click on the box that says "Demonstration," and then choose "Take a Demo Test" from the choices at the top of the screen. On the bottom of the same screen, click on "I wish to proceed," and on the next page that comes up, choose "Weight IAT."

In school. As a teenager, much of your time is spent in school, and not all of that time is spent with your nose in a book. Although academic in purpose, schools are social places where kids and teens learn how to interact with one another, form social networks, and create and foster friendships. Unfortunately, school can be a tough place for teens who are overweight or obese.

Studies show that many overweight adolescents and teens are less accepted socially, were not considered as important as other members of their social networks, and had fewer friendships than teens of healthy weight. It even has been discovered and reported by researchers at the Yale University Rudd Center for Food Policy and Obesity, a research and public-policy organization, that some teachers have less regard for students who are obese than those who aren't.

Obese or overweight teens may be excluded, either overtly or subtly, from clubs, activities, and sports, and may face teasing and ridicule during activities such as gym or swimming instruction. A study of nearly 5,000 students in grades 7 to 12 in public middle and high schools in the Minneapolis/Saint Paul metropolitan area revealed that 30 percent of girls and 25 percent of boys who participated in the study reported being teased by peers.

Teasing and ridicule among teenagers is neither new nor restricted to overweight kids, but teens who are obese are more likely to experience teasing than those who are not. Teasing of any sort can be hurtful and increase the risk of poor *body image,* low *self-esteem,* and depression. When those things occur, it sets the teen up for further stigma.

At home. It's nice to think of home as a place where you're accepted and loved just the way you are, but it's not uncommon for family members to criticize and exhibit bias toward a child or sibling who is overweight or obese. In the same study mentioned above, nearly 30 percent of girl participants and 16 percent of boy participants reported weight-based teasing at home.

Teasing at home can have the same results as school-based teasing, and, in some ways, can be even more hurtful because it can be perceived as a betrayal of trust. Discovery of the degree of weight-based teasing that occurs at home has come as a surprise to some researchers, who were previously unaware of its prevalence.

On the job. *Weight-based discrimination* at work is well documented. Overweight job applicants are viewed less favorably than those who aren't overweight, and are less likely to be hired, despite having the same qualifications and experience. Once hired, overweight and obese workers can expect to earn less and get fewer promotions than their thinner peers.

The Rudd Center reports that "studies have found that overweight employees are considered lazy, sloppy, less competent, lacking in self-discipline, disagreeable, less conscientious, and poor role models."

While the issue of weight-based job discrimination is attracting increasing attention, it has not yet been addressed legally on a widespread basis. There are no federal laws to protect employees

The Minnesota study revealed the frightening statistic that teens who are teased for their weight both in school and at home suffer very serious emotional effects. About half of the girls in that group reported having suicidal thoughts, and one-fourth had attempted suicide. For boys, 34 percent reported suicidal thoughts and 12 percent had attempted suicide. All parents and teachers should be aware of those statistics.

from weight-based job discrimination, and few state or local laws. Michigan and the District of Columbia have regulations in place, and Massachusetts has a bill pending to establish regulations. Of course, these regulations, as useful as they can be, will not magically erase people's biases, and job discrimination is likely to continue for some years.

When you need medical care. Sadly, even some health care workers are not exempt from feelings of bias against obese patients. Studies have shown that obese patients feel they are treated less respectfully than others, and sometimes experience delays in care. They are more likely to cancel appointments or put off preventive services, citing negative attitudes toward them from health care providers, embarrassment at having to be weighed, and other reasons.

Weight bias among health care workers runs the full gamut, including doctors, nurses, medical students, psychologists, dieticians, and even obesity specialists. Fortunately, there is a growing awareness of this problem among members of the medical community, and increasing attention on the need for sensitivity when treating obese patients.

COPING WITH SOCIETAL STIGMA AND MISUNDERSTANDING OF OBESITY

Everyone who has ever been teased or bullied knows that it can be annoying, frustrating, and downright hurtful. When you face outright discrimination in addition to teasing, the situation becomes compounded and even more difficult to deal with.

Teasing and bullying can range from exclusion from social groups and name-calling to public humiliation. One girl reported on a teen obesity forum that she was pushed to the ground and held down by two people while a boy pulled up her shirt and poked sticks into her skin while calling her names and laughing. If you are teased or bullied, the most important thing to remember is that you do not deserve that sort of behavior, and it is not your fault. The person or people bullying you may be doing so because they're desperate to make themselves look good or important, or even because they are targets of bullying or abuse themselves and are reacting in anger toward someone else. While that doesn't make bullying easier to take, it might help you to better understand why it occurs.

If you have been teased or bullied at school because of your weight, or you suspect or fear that you will be, consider these suggestions from the Rudd Center for Food Policy and Obesity:

If you're the parent of an obese or overweight child who is being teased or bullied, it's imperative that you are your child's ally. If you have engaged in any sort of teasing of your child, stop immediately, and do not permit other family members to tease. If problems are occurring in school, talk to the principal or guidance counselor about the situation and ask what can be done. Remember that it's important to emphasize health while de-emphasizing weight. Advocate a healthy approach by providing healthy meals and snacks and encouraging children, whether or not they are overweight, to get plenty of physical activity.

- Don't fight back or retaliate. Bullies are trying to upset you so you'll react. If you refuse to do that by remaining calm and ignoring them, you deny them their fun and the game becomes boring. As soon as you're able, remove yourself from the scene.
- Project a feeling of confidence. Keep you chin up and stand tall. Be aware of your surroundings and try to look sure of yourself. This will make you less of a target for teasing or bullying.
- Stick with a buddy. Bullies are more likely to target someone who is alone than someone who is with another person or a group.
- Stand up for somebody else who is being bullied. It's the right thing to do, it establishes you as a brave person, and you might make a good friend in the process.
- Talk to a trusted adult, whether it's someone at school, a parent, a counselor, or whoever. Bullying is a serious problem and should not be tolerated. Trust that an adult will want to help you.

If you're experiencing teasing at home or from a friend, try these strategies as suggested by the Rudd Center:

- Tell your friends and family members that their words or actions are hurtful to you, and in no way helpful. Let them know that when they comment about your weight, it makes you feel bad and doesn't motivate you in a positive way.

▶ Help to educate your friends and family members about health behaviors by suggesting that you take a walk together, or cook a healthy meal. You could find some healthy recipes on the Internet and suggest making them together. Teach your family and friends that being overweight doesn't mean you aren't concerned about your health.

Hopefully, society will become increasingly aware of the problem of weight-based bias and discrimination, and measures will be taken to fight these. We can all help by working to educate others about the problem and helping them to understand that obesity is a complicated condition with many causes, not a simple matter of self-control or willpower.

PSYCHOLOGICAL IMPACTS OF OVERWEIGHT AND OBESITY

Nearly all teenagers struggle with self-identity and self-esteem as they navigate complex social networks and try to find their places within them. It's not unusual to wonder about exactly who you are and where you're heading in life. It can be difficult to figure out where you fit in, who are your real friends, and what will be your eventual role in the greater society. Teenagers, regardless of their weight, face many pressures and tend to experience frequent discomfort and self-consciousness. In plain language, the teen years aren't easy for anyone, even for those who appear to "have it all."

For teens who are coping with obesity, however, those years can be especially rough and challenging.

We live in a society in which thin women and fit, athletic men are held up as the ideal. We hear and read from childhood that in order to be considered attractive we should be thin. And, in some segments of our society, our obsession with thinness continues even as society's pants size increases.

As a result, those who don't fulfill societal expectations of thinness often end up feeling that there must be something wrong with them, or that they're less attractive than thin people. Many people, including doctors, parents, teachers, and others—many of whom don't fit "the ideal figure," themselves—understand that these expectations to be thin and athletic are unfair and unrealistic. Wise and experienced people understand that beauty is not measured in a waist size, and that the "ideal" man or woman comes in all different colors, shapes, and sizes.

Oprah Winfrey, who is greatly admired and arguably one of the most influential women in the world, has struggled with her weight for years, without letting it get in the way of her success or satisfaction about herself. Perhaps Oprah understands that one's value is not restricted to how he or she looks, but at what one accomplishes and contributes to the good of society. Your weight is only one part of who you are. Consider, and encourage others to consider, all that is you—including your intelligence, your activities, how you interact with others, and your hopes for the future.

Still, weight-based stigma is prevalent, and teens and others who are judged by how much they weigh frequently suffer significant psychological consequences. Some teens become obsessed with appearance to the point that they develop eating disorders in their attempt to gain social acceptance.

HOW BODY IMAGE AFFECTS SELF-ESTEEM

Many factors can affect a person's self-esteem, which is the attitude that one has regarding oneself. A language impediment, severe acne, a physical disability, a family situation, ethnic background, sexual orientation, and many other conditions and circumstances contribute how a person might feel about himself or herself. As you may already know, weight and body image can also be factors in how you perceive yourself.

A recent study from the University of North Carolina at Chapel Hill suggests that many teens have trouble separating how they feel about their bodies with how they feel about themselves as people. Those who don't like their bodies, for whatever reasons, often have trouble liking themselves.

Researchers who have studied the possible connection between obesity and lowered self-esteem have discovered some interesting facts. For example, results vary among boys and girls, and among teens of different races and socioeconomic groups. The self-esteem of girls is more closely linked with body image than that of boys. And differences in attitude regarding weight among various cultures and races affect how members of those cultures and races think about their bodies, and also their levels of self-esteem.

Kids and teens who are teased about their weight, either by family members or peers or both, are more likely to suffer from poor body image and low self-esteem. They also are more likely to experience depression and consider suicide, research shows.

COPING WITH DEPRESSION

Everyone feels sad and down at times—it's a normal part of life. Sometimes, though, feelings of sadness or despair don't go away, but become so pronounced that they interfere with a person's daily life. Those feelings might be so strong that they get in the way of sleeping, eating, relationships, and concentrating on schoolwork or other activities.

The National Institute of Mental Health describes depression, also called clinical depression, as "when the blues don't go away," and lists 11 common symptoms. Depression affects people differently, however, and not everyone who is depressed experiences all or even most of the following symptoms:

> ➤ Ongoing sad, anxious, or empty feelings
> ➤ Feelings of hopelessness
> ➤ Feelings of guilt, worthlessness, or helplessness
> ➤ Feeling irritable or restless
> ➤ Loss of interest in activities or hobbies that were once enjoyable, including sex

There are numerous resources available for those suffering from depression or wondering if they're suffering from depression. A more complete listing of resources is included in an appendix in the back of this book, but a good place to begin if you're looking for help or to figure out if you are indeed suffering from depression is the National Foundation for Depressive Illness, which provides a recorded announcement of the signs of depression and offers suggestions for getting help. The 24-hour service can be reached by calling (800) 248-4344.

If you're suffering from depression, you're in good company. About 19 million people experience depression every year, according to the National Institutes of Health, and the majority of those people don't receive the help they need. Depression affects people of both sexes and of every race, ethnic background, and socioeconomic group. A few of the many well known people who have suffered from depression include Albert Einstein, astronaut Buzz Aldrin, hip-hop artist Kool Keith, author J. K. Rowling of Harry Potter fame, actress Brooke Shields, and singer Janet Jackson.

- Feeling tired all the time
- Difficulty concentrating, remembering details, or making decisions
- Not able to go to sleep or stay asleep (insomnia); may wake in the middle of the night, or sleep all the time
- Overeating or loss of appetite
- Thoughts of suicide or making suicide attempts
- Ongoing aches and pains, headaches, cramps, or digestive problems that do not go away

If you are experiencing some or all of these symptoms and you believe you are suffering from depression, it's very, very important that you discuss your situation with a parent, the school nurse, your doctor, a community counselor, or other adult who cares about you and will assist you in getting help.

We don't fully understand why some people become depressed while others don't. There's evidence that some types of depression run in families, and that brain chemistry and structure are factors in depression. Environmental and psychological stresses, such as the loss of a loved one, a traumatic event, the loss of a job, and poor relationships with others also are thought to trigger depression in some people, but sometimes depression occurs with no clear triggering event, affecting those who appear to have everything going for themselves. When that happens, the depressed person may feel very guilty about his condition, and may be stigmatized by others, causing the depression to become even worse. Anyone suffering from depression should understand that it's not his fault, and the condition is not something to feel guilty about. The smartest thing to do if you believe you're suffering from depression, regardless of what anyone else says, is to ask for professional help. Depression is a serious health issue, but it often can be treated very well. Don't assume or let someone else tell you that how you're feeling is just a "stage" you're going through, or that you can "pull yourself out of it."

The good news is that, while depression is a serious illness, it's common and treatable. Most doctors prefer a combination of psychotherapy (counseling) and medication for treating depression. The length of treatment will vary, depending on the severity of the illness and other factors.

Many people who have suffered severe depression have received treatment and are again enjoying life and feeling hopeful and happy.

One of the major risks of depression among teens is suicide. Suicide is the third leading cause of death among young people between the ages of 15 and 24, and the sixth leading cause for those between five and 14, according to the American Academy of Child & Adolescent Psychiatry. If you have thoughts of harming yourself, or know someone else who does, it is absolutely imperative to tell someone who can help. Early symptoms of suicide are listed by the National Institutes of Health as: depression, statements or expressions of guilt feeling, tension or anxiety, nervousness, and impulsiveness. Critical signs that a person may be getting ready to make a suicide attempt are: sudden change in behavior, especially calmness after a period of anxiety; giving away belongings or attempting to settle issues; direct or indirect references to suicide; direct attempts at suicide. If you or someone you know is considering suicide, ask a family member or friend to help you and do not leave their presence until you have received professional help. If no one is available to help you, call your doctor or call 911. The National Suicide Prevention Lifeline has a toll-free, 24-hour hotline that is staffed by trained counselors. The number is (800) 273-TALK [8255].

Depression is nothing to be ashamed about. It affects millions of teens every year and, as stated earlier, is a treatable condition.

UNDERSTANDING AND AVOIDING RISKY BEHAVIORS

Risky behaviors are intentional actions that may result in harm or lead to harm. These behaviors include using drugs or alcohol, engaging in unsafe sexual activity, driving after drinking or drug use, driving too fast, not using seat belts, engaging in violent activities, possessing a weapon, or participating in other dangerous pursuits.

Engaging in risky behaviors is not uncommon among teenagers. What you have to remember, however, is that they're not called risky behaviors for no reason, and that grave safety, health, and legal consequences can result from participating in these sorts of activities.

Researchers have concluded that there is a link between risky behaviors and depression, and that teens who exhibit risky behaviors are more likely to experience depression than those who do not, and vice versa.

If you are engaging in risky behaviors, or are tempted to participate, and experiencing symptoms of depression, do not lose any time in contacting a responsible adult who can help you. It's a good idea to talk to someone if you think you have a tendency toward risky behavior, even if you aren't practicing those behaviors. Obese teens who feel unconnected or that they don't belong sometimes may be tempted to participate in risky behaviors because they think their actions will win them acceptance or help them to fit in, or because they like how the activity makes them feel. A teen who is being pressured might agree to have sex, or even unsafe sex, with someone in an attempt to get that person to like her. Or, a teen who drinks might act less inhibited and feel that he's better able to fit in with a certain group.

Think carefully about the possible results of engaging in risky behavior. Not only would getting arrested for drug use or drunken driving negatively impact your ability to be hired for certain jobs, but risky behavior increases the likelihood that you—or someone else— will be injured or killed. Teens tend to feel invincible, like nothing bad can possibly happen to them. That's actually part of the normal psychological and personality development process of teenagers. A look at the newspaper or TV news, however, readily shows that teens are no more invincible than anyone of any other age, and that car crashes and other accidents or violence injure and kill teens daily. Avoiding risky behaviors is the best policy.

INCREASING CONCERN ABOUT MEDICAL EFFECTS OF OBESITY IN CHILDREN AND TEENS

Obesity is known to cause complications that can have serious, adverse effects on physical health, and doctors and public-health officials are becoming increasingly concerned about the implications of the increase in obesity. If obesity was simply a matter of excess weight, it wouldn't be of great concern to doctors. It is the health complications that obesity causes that are alarming to the medical community.

As a result, more and more attention is being directed on the health effects of obesity, for teens, kids, and adults. Doctors are becoming increasingly concerned about obesity-related health disorders showing up in children and teens that used to be found almost only in adults.

Obesity-related type 2 diabetes, for instance, has long been called "adult-onset diabetes," because it almost always occurred in adults. Traditionally, children who became diabetic developed the type 1 form of the disease, which is not related to obesity. Increasing numbers of adolescents, however, are developing type 2 diabetes, leaving the medical community to worry that this condition could become a prevalent, chronic disease among this age group. According to the SEARCH for Diabetes in Youth Study Group, 3,700 youth in America are diagnosed with type 2 diabetes each year. While the total incidence of this form of the disease is still relatively low, it is a matter of concern. For various reasons, those belonging to minority groups have a higher chance of developing type 2 diabetes than those who are not minorities.

Conditions that do not have symptoms include high blood pressure, elevated cholesterol and triglycerides, hardening of the arteries, *insulin resistance, metabolic syndrome,* fatty liver, and *left ventricular hypertrophy.* Those that do cause symptoms include gallstones, polycystic ovary syndrome, type 2 diabetes, orthopedic disorders, sleep apnea, and acid reflux disease.

Other health conditions that were once pretty much adult conditions now showing up in teens include high blood pressure, early hardening of the arteries, polycystic ovary syndrome, *sleep apnea*, and nonalcoholic *fatty liver disease*. Some of these conditions have symptoms while others do not. Let's consider the effects these sorts of conditions might cause.

CARDIOVASCULAR DISORDERS

Doctors are seeing big increases in the number of kids and teens suffering from one or more conditions associated with cardiovascular disorders. A big problem is that when conditions such as high blood pressure or elevated cholesterol levels show up at an early age, patients are more likely to experience consequences of those conditions sooner than what would have been considered normal in the past. These cardiovascular disorders do not have symptoms, meaning that you can have high blood pressure, elevated cholesterol, or another condition for a long time without knowing about it. If you haven't been checked for the conditions mentioned above, it's a good idea to ask your doctor about having some tests done.

High blood pressure. Also known as hypertension, high blood pressure causes the heart to work harder to pump blood to the body and contributes to cardiovascular disease, stroke, eye problems, and kidney disease. There usually are no symptoms of high blood pressure, which makes it particularly dangerous. Several factors, including genetics, lack of physical activity, poor diet, and aging, are thought to contribute to hypertension. A doctor or nurse can measure your blood pressure with a device called a sphygmomanometer, which consists of a stethoscope, arm cuff, dial, pump, and valve. You can also get your blood pressure taken at health fairs, at special machines in some drug or grocery stores, or with home blood pressure monitors. High blood pressure can be treated with lifestyle changes and medications, if necessary. People who are susceptible to hypertension should be careful to monitor their blood pressure so it can be kept at an acceptable level.

Elevated cholesterol and/or triglycerides. Cholesterol and triglycerides are types of fats that can accumulate in the body and are linked to cardiovascular disorders, stroke, and other health problems. There are no symptoms. Cholesterol collects in the arteries, and can make it difficult for blood to get to the heart and other important organs. Triglycerides result from excess calories, sugar, or alcohol, and are stored in the body's fat cells. Cholesterol and triglycerides attach to proteins to make their way through the blood. There are several types of cholesterol, but the one that commonly causes problems ("bad cholesterol") by building up as plaque in the arteries is contained in low-density lipoproteins, or LDL. Another type of cholesterol, in high-density lipoproteins, or HDL, actually helps the body to get rid of cholesterol, and is often called "good cholesterol." A blood test is necessary to determine cholesterol and triglyceride levels. Lifestyle changes can result in lower levels of cholesterol and triglycerides, and medication may be prescribed, if necessary.

Left ventricular hypertrophy. This is an increased thickness of the heart's main pumping chamber, and it increases the possibility of heart disease. Left ventricular hypertrophy is not in itself a disease, but it indicates an underlying health problem. Associated with high blood pressure, obesity, and aging, the condition can exist for a long time without any symptoms, and sometimes symptoms never occur. If they do, they're likely to be shortness of breath, chest pain, fainting, irregular heartbeat, and dizziness.

METABOLIC PROBLEMS

Type 2 diabetes, insulin resistance, and metabolic syndrome (which is a whole group of risk factors) can be classified as *metabolic problems.* Insulin resistance and metabolic syndrome increase the chances of developing cardiovascular disease and diabetes.

Type 2 diabetes. A disease such as diabetes can be extremely disruptive. Patients must check their blood glucose levels daily by sticking a finger and depositing a drop of blood on a test strip that gets placed into a meter, pay close attention to when and what they eat, and often need to use oral medications or learn to inject *insulin.* These procedures, which must be done regularly, can be inconvenient and annoying. More concerning is that even minor illnesses like a cold or stomach virus can cause increases in blood glucose and make diabetes more difficult to manage. If not properly managed, diabetes can have serious long-term consequences, including damage to the heart and blood vessels, eyes, kidneys, nerves, and gums and teeth. Symptoms of type 2 diabetes include excessive thirst, unexpected weight loss, nausea, dry mouth, blurred vision, tingling in the hands and feet, frequent urination, and skin, vaginal, or urinary infections. A blood test is necessary to diagnose type 2 diabetes, and it's imperative that the disease be managed carefully in order to avoid the complications mentioned above.

Insulin resistance. This is when cells in the body do not respond as well as normal to insulin, which is a hormone secreted by the pancreas, an organ located behind the stomach. The job of insulin is to remove glucose (a sugar) from the bloodstream so that the glucose can be used by cells for energy. When the body doesn't respond to the insulin that's been released, the pancreas releases more insulin. This results in high levels of insulin in the blood, which together with high sugars can lead to diabetes. Insulin resistance can be difficult to diagnose because there are no symptoms. It is treatable with lifestyle changes and medication, if necessary.

Metabolic syndrome. This isn't a disease in itself, but a group of risk factors that increase chances of heart disease, problems with blood vessels, and diabetes. The risk factors identified for metabolic syndrome are high blood pressure, high blood sugar, high triglyceride levels, low HDL ("good") cholesterol, and excessive abdominal fat. This condition does not have symptoms, and can be difficult to diagnose. Treatment, which includes lifestyle changes and in some cases medication, is targeted at each existing risk factor, such as working to lower blood pressure or triglyceride levels.

PULMONARY CONDITIONS

Obesity has been linked to pulmonary conditions such as asthma and sleep apnea, which can be disruptive and worrisome conditions.

Asthma. A chronic disease that causes narrowing of the airways that carry oxygen to the lungs, asthma can cause discomfort and require frequent treatment. If you've ever had a severe asthma attack, you know it can be scary and distressing, and often requires hospitalization. Asthma is common, affecting 22 million Americans and resulting in 2 million visits each year to emergency rooms. Asthma affects different people in different ways, and not everyone experiences the same symptoms, which include coughing (especially at night), wheezing, shortness of breath, and chest pain or discomfort. It can be difficult to diagnose, because symptoms can mimic the symptoms of other disorders. If your doctor suspects you have asthma, he or she might recommend a pulmonary function test to assess the function of your lungs. Allergy tests also can be used in the diagnosis of asthma. There are many medications available to treat asthma, but the trick to managing the condition successfully is to stay on top of it and treat it as necessary so as to avoid or minimize asthma attacks, which can result in extreme difficulty breathing. Keeping asthma under control as much as possible is the best way to reduce the effect it can have on your life.

Sleep apnea. Obesity also is linked to sleep apnea, which is characterized by irregular breathing, snoring, and poor quality of sleep. People who suffer from sleep apnea often experience significant daytime sleepiness caused by interrupted sleep at night. This can effect school and work performance, and make you less likely to enjoy normal activities. Sleep apnea also can contribute to high blood pressure, stroke, and cardiovascular problems. Anyone can get sleep apnea, which most often is caused by a blockage of the airway that occurs when soft tissue in the back of the throat relaxes during sleep and obstructs breathing. This is called obstructive sleep apnea, and it's more common than central sleep apnea, which occurs when muscles don't receive a message from the brain to breathe. Risk factors for sleep apnea, in addition to being overweight, include being a male, being 40 or older, having a large neck size or large tonsils, and a family history of sleep apnea. It's possible to have sleep apnea and not know it, although there are symptoms, including sore or dry throat upon awakening, gasping for air upon awakening, morning headaches, fatigue and sleepiness during the day, forgetfulness and mood changes, and frequent waking during the night or insomnia. Sleep apnea often is diagnosed with the help of a test that records brain and muscle activity, breathing and snoring, and monitors oxygen levels in the blood and other factors. Sleep apnea tests are conducted in sleep labs, located in hospitals or doctors' office buildings. There are a range of treatments for sleep apnea, including lifestyle changes, wearing a mask to help keep airways open, using dental devices, and even surgery.

ORTHOPEDIC DISORDERS

Blount's disease, slipped capital femoral epiphyses (SCFE), and *osteoarthritis* are orthopedic conditions that have been linked to obesity in both adults and teens.

Blount's disease. This disorder causes a bowlegged appearance and, left untreated, can progress until it becomes difficult or impossible to walk. The condition is treated with braces in young children, and can require surgery if not diagnosed early. It is more common in African-American children than among other groups. A doctor who suspects Blount's disease after examining a child will X-ray the knee and lower leg to determine if it's present. When left untreated, Blount's disease can cause deformity and make activity difficult.

Slipped capital femoral epiphyses (SCFE). This is a disorder of the hip where there is a separation of the ball of the hip joint and the upper end of the thigh bone, or femur. The condition requires surgery, and can be painful and require long recovery periods and difficulty with day-to-day activities. Symptoms generally appear in adolescents and teens between the ages of eight and 16, although the disorder most commonly effects kids between the ages of 11 and 14. Boys experience *slipped capital femoral epiphyses* more often than girls, but symptoms tend to appear earlier in girls. Symptoms include pain in the hip; decreased movement; discomfort in the knee, thigh, or groin while walking or running; stiffness and limping; knee pain; and muscle spasms. SCFE is thought to be caused by rapid growth and hormone imbalances during adolescence, and its onset can be preceded by a rapid increase in height and weight or an injury.

Osteoarthritis. This condition, also called degenerative joint disease, can occur in nearly any joint in the body, but is most common in the knees, hips, and spine. It occurs when cartilage, a rubbery material that covers the end of bones in the joints, breaks down and loses its ability to cushion the joints. In severe cases, the cartilage wears away and bones rub against each other, causing severe pain. The chances of developing osteoarthritis increase with age, when it becomes a very common condition in varying degrees. Symptoms, which develop over time, include soreness, aching, and swelling in the joints; pain in the joints during use or after inactivity; and accumulation of fluid in the joint. Overuse, or in the case of obesity, overcharge of a particular joint, such as a knee, can contribute to the condition, as can an injury to a joint. Obesity increases the risk of osteoarthritis in the knee and hip. The condition is diagnosed by X-rays and other means, and is treated in a variety of ways, ranging from lifestyle changes to medication and surgery. Osteoarthritis can make daily tasks of living such as climbing steps uncomfortable, and can limit activities that you enjoy.

GASTROINTESTINAL DISORDERS

Gastroesophageal reflux, gallstones, and fatty liver disease are becoming increasingly common in teenagers, and are thought to be linked to obesity.

Gastroesophageal reflux. This occurs when stomach contents flow back into the esophagus. It can cause severe pain and discomfort, such as heartburn, and ultimately can damage the esophagus or even cause esophageal cancer. People with reflux disease must often rely on medications and have their condition monitored, as it can be serious. The most common symptom of reflux disease is heartburn, but occasional heartburn does not mean that you have gastroesophageal reflux. If you have frequent heartburn, however, you should ask your doctor about this condition. Often, a doctor who suspects gastroesophageal reflux will prescribe medicine to prevent the stomach contents from moving into the esophagus. If the medicine works, the diagnosis is confirmed. Tests also are available to check for the condition. Many people who develop gastroesophageal reflux will have it for the rest of their lives, but there are ways to manage the condition so that it is less bothersome. Losing even a little bit of weight can decrease symptoms, as can avoiding lying down right after eating, eating several small meals instead of one large one, elevating the head of your bed, and wearing clothes that are loose around the waist.

Gallstones. Gallstones occur when cholesterol and other materials contained in bile, a substance produced by the liver to help digest fats, harden to form stones. They can be tiny or as large as golf balls. People who are overweight or obese tend to be more likely to develop gallstones than those who aren't. Gallstones become a problem when they block a duct and bile backs up. This can be a very painful condition, and accompanied by chills and fever. Sometimes the skin and whites of the eyes will take on a yellow hue. Gallstones also can cause symptoms that result in chest pain, and can mimic a heart attack. Gallstones can be diagnosed by ultrasound, which is an imaging of the inside of your body. If the ultrasound doesn't reveal gallstones, your doctor may opt to do a gall bladder scan, in which dye is injected into your arm and X-rays taken as it moves through your gall bladder and other organs. If gallstones cause severe pain or reoccur, your doctor might advise you to have your gallbladder removed. The gallbladder is a small sac just under the liver where bile is stored. You can live perfectly well without it.

Nonalcoholic fatty liver disease. Nonalcoholic fatty liver disease is another disorder associated with obesity. It is called nonalcoholic fatty liver disease to distinguish it from a similar condition that is associated with excessive alcohol use and alcoholism. Fatty liver disease is the condition of fat deposits in the liver, which can eventually cause inflammation, cirrhosis, and liver failure. While fatty liver disease has no symptoms, liver disease is very serious, sometimes resulting in the need for a liver transplant. A patient can live for years with liver disease without knowing it until the damage has become so severe that it cause problems such as fatigue, weight loss, and weakness. If your doctor suspects you have fatty liver disease, he or she will scan the liver by ultrasound, or an MRI or CT scan. If signs of the disease are present, the doctor may recommend a liver biopsy, in which a tissue sample is taken from the liver and examined. There is no single treatment for fatty liver disease. Instead, it's treated by addressing the underlying causes, such as obesity, insulin resistance, or diabetes.

POLYCYSTIC OVARY SYNDROME

Polycystic ovary syndrome (PCOS) is the leading cause of infertility among women in the United States, and it is linked to obesity. PCOS is categorized by missed or irregular menstrual periods and increased levels of testosterone (a male hormone) in girls. Too much testosterone can cause females to have excess facial and body hair, problems with acne, and even problems with hair loss, with serious emotional implications. These symptoms often first appear during the teen years. PCOS also is related to insulin resistance, which can lead to the onset of type 2 diabetes. The condition is common, affecting up to one out of 10 women in the United States. Lab tests to check blood sugar, insulin, and hormone levels are used to diagnose PCOS, and a

You may have heard that obesity also is associated with various types of cancer, including esophageal, colorectal, breast, endometrial, and kidney cancers. While it's not entirely clear how or why these cancers are associated with obesity, doctors suspect it could be due to hormone imbalance that sometimes occurs in obese patients, or be related to nutritional factors. If you are overweight or obese, it does not mean that you will get cancer. Doctors, however, are concerned about the association, and remind patients that, again, even small changes can result in decreased chances of developing the disease.

pelvic ultrasound may be ordered to check for cysts on the ovaries. Lifestyle changes and some medicines may be used to treat PCOS, and symptoms such as unwanted hair can be cosmetically addressed. Losing even a small amount of weight can improve symptoms of this condition. PCOS can be difficult to endure, and there are some support groups available. WebMD, found online at www.webmd.com, offers a support group, and there may be groups in your community. Check a community bulletin board, often found in daily or weekly newspapers, to learn what's available.

As you can see, obesity is thought to contribute to a variety of medical conditions. Having a serious condition such as cardiovascular disease or diabetes can negatively impact your quality of life.

WHAT YOU NEED TO KNOW

> Obesity can affect you socially, psychologically, and physically.

> Being obese makes a person more likely to experience discrimination, which can affect the schools he'll go to or jobs he'll get, his earnings, his marital status, and his overall quality of life.

> There are strategies you can employ to help you cope with teasing and bullying at home, in school, and in other areas of your life.

> Most teenagers struggle with self-identity and self-esteem, but for obese teens, these years can be especially unpleasant and challenging.

> Obese teens are more likely to suffer from depression than their non-obese peers, and should be encouraged to seek help when necessary, as depression often can be very successfully treated and managed.

> Obese teens must remember that their obesity is just one piece of their identity, and should concentrate on other, positive attributes such as an artistic talent, a caring manner, an aptitude for working with children, or whatever they feel they can be successful at.

> Doctors are increasingly concerned about the consequences of obesity on physical health, particularly when obesity occurs at an early age—and problems are beginning to show up in people at much younger ages than they have in the past. Most of these conditions can be easily diagnosed by your doctor.

Making the Decision to Take Control of Your Health: Be Healthy for Your Own Sake

Cindi had been struggling with her weight for a long time when she finally decided to do something about it. She'd thought about making some changes in the past, but had never gotten around to doing it—until now.

Her health class had just finished a unit on health and weight, during which they'd learned about things like energy balance, keeping food diaries, and the importance of being physically active. Cindi really liked her health teacher, Mrs. Cassidy, and she decided to talk to her about changes she could make to help her be healthier.

Mrs. Cassidy was happy to talk to Cindi, and recommended that Cindi begin by learning all she could about health, obesity, and weight control. She told Cindi about a Web site called BAM! Body and Mind, which contained a lot of helpful information.

Cindi began using BAM! and other sites to learn about how many calories were in different foods, serving sizes, keeping track of what you eat, how advertising can have an effect on what and when you eat, different types of physical activity, and lots of other things.

She took notes on everything she learned and talked to her mom and dad about it. She began making small changes in what she ate and drank, cutting out soda and measuring out portions at dinner. She started keeping food and physical activity diaries, and tracking when and where she was exposed to food advertising. The more she learned, the more interested she became in finding out more.

Soon Cindi began to feel healthier. Her clothes seemed to fit a little bit better, and her parents and friends noticed that she appeared to have more energy and be more positive about things. Sure, there were times when it was really hard to not eat the whole package of cookies, and she still got teased about her weight now and then at school. She still encountered problems, but she felt more in control and better prepared to deal with them.

While there are many rewards to be had from taking control of your health and making the necessary changes to assure that you'll be as healthy as possible, these are not easy tasks. Having said that, however, remember that many people have been successful in finding and employing methods that result in improved health (regardless of weight!) and sometimes even weight loss.

While doctors and researchers are learning more all the time about what causes obesity and how it might be prevented or treated, we do not yet have all the answers. We are still exploring the most effective ways of treating obesity, and many questions remain. Some successful treatment strategies have been identified, however, and that's what we will discuss in this chapter and further in chapter 7.

When it comes right down to it, obesity prevention and treatment depend on you being able and willing to make behavior changes that impact energy balance. In chapter 2 you learned that energy balance is when you use up, or expend, about as many calories as you consume. If you eat about as many calories as it takes for you to stay alive, grow, and participate in daily activities, that's energy balance.

There are ways that you can achieve energy balance, or close to energy balance, but they all require some changes in behavior.

WHAT IS BEHAVIOR CHANGE?

Simply put, *behavior change* is doing things differently from how you have done them in the past. That encompasses a huge spectrum of activities, from changing your shower time from night to morning, doing your homework as soon as you get home instead of waiting until after dinner, walking to school instead of getting a ride with your mom, or drinking water or other unsweetened beverages instead of soda.

Changing behaviors that you've practiced for a long time can be difficult. As human beings, we tend to get comfortable with what we do and how we do it, and sometimes just the thought of changing our behaviors can be worrisome—even frightening.

Every now and then you'll hear about someone who has an experience that causes him or her to dramatically change a behavior. More often, however, behavior change occurs over time. It takes a while for most people to decide that they want to change a behavior, and then to figure out how they'll go about doing so.

There are no ironclad guarantees for achieving behavior change, but there are strategies you can employ to improve your chances of doing so. You'll read more about them in the next section.

LEARNING HOW TO CHANGE BEHAVIOR

If you have decided that you'd like to take charge of your health and make some positive changes to it, give yourself a big pat on the back. Even acknowledging and addressing the issue of your health are important steps. The next thing to do is to begin thinking about what behaviors you may want to change in order to control your weight and achieve better health, and how you can best go about making those changes. Some steps thought to increase the likelihood of behavior change are outlined below.

Increase awareness through self-monitoring and analyzing behaviors. We often are not good at recognizing our own behaviors. You might be very aware, for instance, that the girl who sits across from you in math class has an extremely annoying habit of cracking her gum, but unaware that you have an equally annoying habit of tapping your fingernails on the desk. When it comes to what we eat and the amount of physical activity we get, we tend to be really bad at judging our behaviors. You can, however, increase awareness of these behaviors by monitoring your food intake and activity levels. You can use a diary or make a chart to keep track of how many servings of fruits and vegetables you eat each day, how much TV you watch, how many minutes of physical activity you complete, how many steps you take (using a pedometer), and so forth. Many doctors recommend that you keep a detailed food diary, listing every single thing you eat or drink, right down to the number of pretzels you grab from the bag to how many ounces of milk you pour onto your cereal. It is also useful to convert these foods into calories and add up how many calories you consume at each meal and over the course of a day. You will be very surprised at how some foods you think are high in calories are not, and others that you think are healthy are actually packed with calories. You'll read a lot more about keeping count of calories in chapter 7, and learn about some good sources that can help you keep track of how many calories you consume. Keeping track of all these sorts of behaviors will make you more aware of them, and can provide an important tool for assessing the changes you want to make. *Self-monitoring* has been clearly shown to increase the chances of losing weight and maintaining weight loss.

Self-monitoring is an important weight-loss tool that works in different ways. A number of proven studies have shown that obese children and adults who practice self-monitoring are more successful at losing weight and at maintaining long-term weight management than those who don't self-monitor. And we've learned that a person who is successful in losing weight often achieves an increased sense of control over his behavior and his ability to control his weight, which leads to even more willingness to self-monitor behavior!

Set and document achievable goals. Goal setting is an important strategy for behavior change, but it should be done in an achievable manner. We know that achieving weight loss involves two types of lifestyle behaviors: dietary and physical activity. Once you've assessed your behaviors in those areas, you'll be able to set some goals to help you achieve change. Let's say that for two weeks you used a pedometer to measure how many steps you take each day. At the end of that time, you figure out that you take an average of 6,000 steps each day. At that point, it may be reasonable for you to set a goal of increasing your daily steps to 8,000 a day, and to come up with some strategies to be able to do so successfully and to continue doing so. Most goals are easy to achieve for a short time. The trick is to set doable goals that you'll be able to achieve and maintain.

Many people find that it's beneficial to set smaller goals that, over time, add up to larger goals. If you currently drink six sodas a day, for instance, your first goal may be to reduce your intake to five a day for two weeks. After that, you cut back to four sodas a day for another two weeks, and so on, until you've reached your final goal of drinking only water or other unsweetened beverages instead of soda. Goals should be written down and checked often. If it becomes clear you've set a goal that's impossible to reach, don't fret if you change it to make it realistic. Every small step will empower you to address bigger change in the future. Some professionals feel that using contracts can help to keep you on track and provide a framework for rewarding positive behavior changes. You might enter into a contract with a parent or a friend, for instance, who agrees to provide a reward in exchange for certain behavior changes you agree to make. If you do it on your own, remember to reward yourself as well. Most people are too harsh on themselves and see only the half-empty glass. If you achieved your goal just five days out of the week, don't get stuck on the two days that you didn't. Celebrate those five days, knowing you reached the goal five days more than you had in the weeks before you decided to make these changes!

Create an environment that's conducive to success. If you're constantly tempted by high-calorie foods or distracted by a TV that's always turned on, your efforts at behavior change are likely to be hindered. If, on the other hand, your refrigerator holds a supply of ready-to-eat fruits and vegetables and other healthy foods, and the TV has been moved out of your bedroom, chances are you'll eat those available foods and find something to do other than sit in front of the television. Think of how, as we discussed in chapter 4, you can create an environment that works for you—not against you—in your efforts to change behaviors. If necessary, set rules for yourself, such as resolving to eat only in the kitchen, or saying "no thanks" when your friends ask you to go along to the fast-food place (but not if they're going to play tennis or shoot hoops). Write down the rules you establish and refer to them when you feel your resolve slipping. Having a plan for what you'll do when something occurs that threatens to derail your efforts can prepare you and make it easier to avoid such a situation. If you know your aunt will insist that you eat a piece of the chocolate cake she made because she *always* insists that you do so, you could politely refuse by saying something like, "You know I love your chocolate cake, but I just ate lunch and am not at all hungry." Help her understand that she can show her love by supporting you in your effort to become healthier, rather than by feeding you. And be prepared for situations where there will be pressure for you to eat. Have you ever tried to turn down a piece of birthday cake, or a second helping of stuffing at Thanksgiving? It's not easy, right? If you anticipate you'll be in a situation where you'll be tempted to eat more than you want to, plan ahead for how to handle it. If you have an idea of what foods will be served, do some calorie exploring. Calculate about how many calories a piece of that birthday cake contains and figure out if having a piece of cake fits into your daily calorie goal. If so, be sure to avoid the table with the chips and peanuts, and have only the cake. Eat it slowly and enjoy every mouthful.

Give yourself feedback on how you're doing and seek it from others when necessary. Chances are that you'll begin to feel better about your health as soon as you've made the decision to take

While working to change behaviors and make positive changes affecting your health, it's important to be aware of "triggers" that can get you off course and cause you to revert to your old behaviors. If you and your friend Terry *always* stop for milk shakes on your way home from school on Wednesdays, you're going to have to figure out how to avoid letting that tradition wreck your plan for behavior change. If Terry is willing, take another route from school so that you don't pass the shake place. Or establish a new Wednesday tradition, like working out to an exercise DVD or volunteering to tutor younger kids.

control and begin working to change some behaviors. If you begin to lose weight, you might notice that your clothes fit a little more comfortably, or that you can walk up that hill near your house without getting quite so out of breath. Your energy level might improve, or you might just feel better about yourself. Others may also notice and provide positive reinforcement through encouraging comments they offer. Keeping track of your weight is an important form of self-monitoring, and studies suggest that it's an important tool in maintaining weight loss. Most doctors recommend that you weigh yourself at around the same time each week, and be sure to keep a record of how many pounds you've lost. You can make a simple chart or graph to help you keep track.

An important aspect to remember is that behavior modification often becomes easier once you've done it for a while. You should continue to use self-monitoring, however, even as your new behaviors begin to feel more like habits. Most people who are successful at maintaining healthier behaviors continue to self-monitor for a very long time, even as their behaviors become more and more established and easier to maintain. Passing on the cookies or potato chips and picking up an apple or handful of baby carrots can become something that you do almost automatically—out of habit. It takes time, and there no doubt will be occasions when you'll succumb to the call of the chocolate chips and go for the cookies instead of the carrots. However, positive behaviors can be established just as negative ones can, making it easier to stick with them.

FINDING THE SUPPORT YOU NEED

While some people can be quite successful at changing behaviors on their own, most of us find that we do better with a little help. Support can range from participating in counseling sessions with a professional to seeking encouragement from a support person. Let's have a look at some options for support that may help you to change behaviors and result in weight loss.

*A **support person.*** Perhaps you know someone who also has decided to make positive changes toward improving his or her health. If so, you may want to think about teaming up in a weight loss partnership. Some people experience great success with partnering with one person, while others are not comfortable with that situation.

As with any successful partnership, you and your *support person* would work together and encourage each other in your efforts. You might discuss your goals and accomplishments, and help each other to get back on track in the event of a slipup. You might choose to participate in physical activities together, to prepare healthy meals together, or to share your food diaries.

You don't need to have a designated support person in order to make successful changes, but it definitely helps.

Family and friends. Studies have made it clear that young people are more successful at changing behaviors and losing weight when they receive support from family and friends. Whether teens like to admit it or not, parents significantly influence their behaviors, both positively and negatively. Those who support their sons' and daughters' efforts to lose weight by encouraging them and providing healthful foods and environments conducive to achieving energy balance can promote positive change. Those who don't, perhaps by not taking into consideration their own eating habits, continuing to offer high-calorie foods, or not encouraging physical activity, can actually discourage their children from changing unhealthy behaviors.

Remember the example given a little earlier about avoiding your aunt's best efforts to get you to eat a piece of cake? Some families—either intentionally or unintentionally—actually make it harder for teens to change behaviors and achieve weight loss.

This can occur for a variety of reasons. Maybe your mom feels bad for you because she thinks you're being deprived. She may urge you to "just this once" go ahead and have that bowl of ice cream like you used to. Sometimes a family member might try to sabotage your efforts because she feels jealous that you've decided to take control of your health and make positive changes, while she tried to do the same thing in the past and wasn't successful. A brother or sister might try to find out how determined you are to succeed, or

Dos and Don'ts for Family Members

Dos: Do be positive and supportive. Compare notes with and get positive suggestions from members of other families in which someone is working to lose weight. Maintain a relaxed home environment. Do ignore and forgive lapses, and instead of calling out your son or brother eating a cookie, catch him doing the right thing. Saying something like, "I noticed that you chose not to take a second helping of meat loaf today. That was great, and I'm really impressed with your strength," goes a long way in helping. Do ask how else you can help. Participate in physical activity with the family member. Being a good role model by modeling the behaviors your family member is trying to achieve has been shown to be a key to your family member's success. You'll be helping by—literally—walking the walk, rather than just talking the talk. Cultivate new interests with the family member losing weight. Do assist your child with measuring portion sizes, counting calories, and perform-ing other weight loss–related tasks as necessary. Some teens are more able and motivated to perform these chores than others. You can help by providing assistance when needed. Do provide frequent praise.

Don'ts: Don't hide food from the person losing weight. Don't threaten or coerce, or avoid social situations out of embarrassment for your fam-ily member or fear that he or she will slip up and eat too much. Do not expect perfection or the achievement of unrealistic goals. Don't lecture, criticize, or reprimand the family member losing weight, and don't play the role of victim or martyr. Don't expect your teen or sibling to avoid all unhealthy foods if the house is full of them, or if that's what everyone else is eating. You can help by limiting the availability of junk food and being sensitive to your teen's weight loss efforts. Don't deny your child certain foods or second helpings, even though denial might seem like the most direct way to help her achieve weight loss. Doing so is likely to cause her to feel angry and resentful, and will limit her ability to learn on her own how to make good decisions concerning food choices.

just try to have a little fun at your expense, by tempting you with unhealthy foods.

If your family has changed its eating habits in order to be supportive and make it easier for you, some members could resent that. If Tuesdays had been pizza night for as long as anyone could remember, and now Tuesdays are soup and salad night, there could be someone in your family who's disappointed with that change—and blames you for it.

Sometimes family members set unrealistic expectations and express disappointment when you don't realize their goals. It's very important that you communicate with your family and help them to understand what you wish to achieve and how you plan to do so.

While it's true that in some cases family members and friends actually can make your task of improving your health more difficult, in most cases, your family and friends will applaud your efforts and provide support as you work to change behaviors and lose weight. If you can't find help in your immediate family, perhaps you have a friend, or a boyfriend or girlfriend, an uncle or aunt, a godparent, or even a teacher who cares enough about you to be your primary source of support and encouragement. Studies have indicated that many people are more successful with losing weight and keeping it off when they pair up with someone with similar goals or someone who is truly engaged with their efforts.

And your family and friends can help to keep you motivated and on track simply by offering words of encouragement and praise.

SEEKING HELP FROM PROFESSIONALS

As the problem of obesity among kids and teens gains national attention and causes increasing concern, more attention is being focused on how to best address and treat obesity.

Once you've decided to take control of your health and make some behavior changes in order to improve it, you may find that you'd benefit from some professional help. You'll learn a lot more about treatments for obesity in the next chapter. Right now, it's important to know that there are people and programs to help you get started.

A physician. As you read in chapter 1, your family doctor is a good starting point. The doctor might help you to work out a treatment plan, establish a regular schedule of visits, or may refer you to a weight loss specialist or to other reliable resources in your community, such as weight loss programs based at a YMCA or a recreational center. If you don't have a family doctor or can't afford the cost of seeing a doctor, check to see if there's a clinic or community health center in your area (findahealthcenter.hrsa.gov). Hospitals also often establish clinics within the communities in which they're located. It's especially important to consult with a doctor if you've experienced any health problems such as those described in chapter 5, and to get readings on blood pressure, cholesterol, and other factors.

An adolescent psychiatrist. If you're experiencing emotional problems in addition to obesity, as is the case for many obese adolescents, an *adolescent psychiatrist* or counselor can work with your physician to put together a treatment plan addressing your weight and your state of mind.

Support groups. Many people find motivation and support from conferring with others who also are trying to improve their health through weight loss. That's one of the reasons why programs that include group meetings are popular. They provide a source of support, in addition to direction on food intake and physical activity. A program such as Weight Watchers, where participants are urged to check in weekly to be weighed and attend an informational session, also tend to help keep participants motivated.

A registered dietician or nutritionist. Someone in this position can help to educate you about appropriate portion sizes, fat and calorie contents of foods, nutrition, and other important topics. There are nutritionists who practice privately, and others associated with hospitals, weight loss centers, and clinics. Just to be sure to find someone who is licensed, certified, or registered, as regulations concerning the education and training of nutritionists vary from state to state. You can find one through the American Dietetic Association's Web site (eatright.org), which has a "Find a Nutrition Professional" feature.

While a nutritionist can help you better understand food-related matters, however, he or she may not be familiar with methods of implementing behavior change. That means that while a nutritionist can supply you with important information, it's likely that you'll also need the behavioral modification methods described above.

UNDERSTANDING HOW BEHAVIOR CHANGE OCCURS

Most experts agree that behavior change usually occurs over a period of time—not as a sudden occurrence. People normally move through several stages before they are ready to commit to making any type of lifestyle change. Researchers use various models to describe the steps of behavior change, some of which are described below. Don't be intimidated by what might appear to be complicated language or abstract ideas. These theories are described just to let you know that they exist, and to give you a starting point if you wish to learn more about them. Some good reading sources are listed in the appendix in the back of this book if you're interested in learning more about behavior change or the theories associated with it.

A popular model to describe behavior change is called the *transtheoretical model of change,* which outlines stages a person may go through on the way to successful behavior change. Not everyone agrees that the transtheoretical model is applicable to weight loss, but it is commonly used. The stages, which also can be applied to other behavior changes such as quitting smoking, are described below.

> ➤ Precontemplation stage: This is the period before you even begin to consider making changes to your behavior. You are not yet ready at this stage to even address the need to change.
> ➤ Contemplation stage: Now you're juggling the pros and cons of changing a behavior or behaviors. You're aware that it would be beneficial to your health to lose some weight, and you've started thinking that giving up soda would be a good step to take toward that goal. The thing is, you really like soda, and you know that you'd miss that big fountain drink that you buy on the way home from school every day. You're not yet ready to make the change, but you're thinking.
> ➤ Preparation stage: At this point, you're getting more serious about making the change and you're taking some steps to get ready to do it. Maybe you've cut back from the 64-ounce soda to the 48-ounce as you get ready to give it up altogether.
> ➤ Action stage: Congratulations, you've done it! Your after-school drink of choice is now a bottle of calorie-free flavored water, and you're saving yourself 600 calories a day by not drinking the two-quart soda.
> ➤ Maintenance and relapse prevention: This is an ongoing stage during which you maintain—or try to maintain—the behavior change or changes that you've made.

Not everyone progresses in an orderly fashion through these stages, and there's no prescribed time period. One person might think about making a change for years before finally doing it, while someone else might contemplate for only a couple of weeks. The listing above is just to help you understand that real change occurs gradually, and is not an instantaneous event.

While the transtheoretical model may be used in weight loss treatment, many models have been put into place to describe pathways leading to behavior change. Some of them are briefly described below.

Behavioral economics theory. Basically, this theory states that, if an apple costs 50 cents, and an ice cream cone costs $5, you're more likely to buy the apple than the ice cream. The *behavioral economics theory* has been applied to studies that demonstrate people are more likely to choose healthier foods when the prices of less healthy foods are increased, or less healthy foods are unavailable. The behavioral economics theory also describes how frequently behaviors go together, and how changing one behavior can change another. For example, watching TV often goes hand-in-hand with eating snacks, such as potato chips. So, if you decide that you will no longer watch TV on Saturday afternoon, you're likely to find that you lose that bag of chips, as well.

Social learning theory. If you spend most of your time with friends or family members who think a day is not complete without a trip to the local fast-food restaurant, you're more likely to also eat fast food than you would if you hung out with folks who concentrated on eating healthier meals and avoided fast food. The *social learning theory* can be applied to the conversation earlier about why social support is so important in weight loss and how what we do is influenced by what we think our friends and family consider to be "normal."

Learning theory. *Learning theory* states that behaviors that result in positive consequences are more likely to be maintained than behaviors that result in negative consequences. For young kids, this may mean they continue to eat fruit instead of potato chips if they are repeatedly praised for making that choice. A reward for teens could be a compliment from a friend, or an enhanced feeling of wellness.

Social ecological model. The *social ecological model* makes the case that behavioral choices are dependent on our interactions with others over a period of time, and that the choices we make are affected by those with whom we interact.

Diffusion theory. *Diffusion theory* applies to how technological ideas expand from being created to being used within society. Person-to-person communication is very important in diffusing information about new technology, some of which is related to weight-control behavior changes.

BEING PREPARED FOR SETBACKS

Regardless of how motivated you feel and committed you are to making behavioral changes that will result in weight loss and improved health, you'll need to be realistic about the possibility that somewhere along the way you'll get off track and fall back into your old behaviors. It might be the chocolate cake at your aunt's birthday party, the pizza at the after-school meeting you attend, or the unexpected stop at the fast-food restaurant with your friends. It might be that one day at the convenience store, for a reason you don't even understand, you pass right by the no-calorie flavored water and fill up a 64-ounce cup at the soda machine. Often, these lapses are triggered by strong emotions. You may feel bad because something unpleasant or even devastating happened that day and you look to food for comfort. Or you may want to celebrate a great achievement with a fun meal and not even think about calories. The important thing, however, isn't that you experience setbacks, but how you deal with them when they occur.

The challenge when you hit a tough spot is to not beat yourself up over it, and to not let it derail your greater efforts. Realistic weight-loss programs always allow for a little flexibility and take into account that everyone gets sidetracked on occasion. What you need to remember is that drinking a big soda instead of water on Tuesday doesn't mean you should, or need to, go back to drinking it every day. Maybe you will need to make a bigger effort than usual on Wednesday and Thursday, but you can probably get back on track in a few days. It also doesn't mean that just because you find yourself off track you might as well throw in the towel and spend the day eating everything that you've managed to stay away from for the past weeks or months.

Slipups are tricky because they tend to cause you to feel bad, making you more prone to another slipup. You might feel really guilty and upset with yourself about eating that double cheeseburger and large order of fries—so guilty and upset, in fact, that you think, "What the heck, I've already messed up, I might as well forget the whole thing."

To avoid that scenario, you can do one of two things. You can make sure that you never slip up, or you can learn strategies that give you control of the situation and get you back on track when you do slip up.

Since the first option is not realistic, it's important that you know how to react in a manner that puts you in the driver's seat and helps you to move past your setback and get back on track. You'll learn more about these strategies in chapter 8, "A Long-Term Approach for Achieving and Maintaining a Healthy Weight."

If you slip up and are having trouble getting back on track, think about what you have already achieved and all the effort you have put in this, and think about what you may need to change or reinstate. If you've fallen behind in keeping your food journal or writing down your goals and tracking progress, get back to it. Talk to your doctor or counselor, or ask a parent to help you by making sure healthy foods are readily accessible.

Just remember that everyone runs into rough spots, but that, when you think positively and don't get discouraged, you can move around those spots and get back on the road to improved health.

WHAT YOU NEED TO KNOW

> Obesity treatment ultimately requires that you are able and willing to make behavior changes that impact energy balance.

> There are steps you can take, such as starting to write down everything you eat and the physical activity that you do, and setting and documenting achievable goals, that can increase your chances of successful behavior change.

> Support from family and friends, and sometimes professionals such as doctors and nutritionists, can help you to be successful in changing behaviors to improve your health.

> There are many theories about how and why behavior change occurs. Most experts believe, however, that behavior change generally occurs over time and is more sustainable when it is progressive. Everyone advances through stages of behavior change at his or her own rate.

> Changing a behavior or behaviors is not easy, and most people experience setbacks along the way. The key is to not get discouraged and to employ strategies that will help you get back on track as quickly as possible.

7

Changing Behaviors to Achieve a Healthy Lifestyle

Angie's weight was closing in on 220 pounds: Her family doctor finally took her mother aside and advised her that Angie needed to get some help. Her blood pressure was elevated, she had high levels of cholesterol and triglycerides, and it was increasingly difficult for her to go up the steps without getting out of breath. It was time to make some changes.

The doctor referred Angie to a specialized center that offered a comprehensive treatment program for obese adolescents and teens. Angie was reluctant to go at first, but she knew that she wanted to feel better, so she agreed.

Angie met with a physician, a psychologist, a social worker, and dietitian. She had a physical examination and a psychological evaluation. The social worker was friendly, and talked to her about school, her friends, and her home life. The dietitian helped her to understand energy balance and the nutritional values of different foods. Together, they figured out how many calories Angie would need to consume in a day in order to stop her weight gain.

Angie attended group sessions one night a week with other teens, during which they talked about what types of physical activity they enjoyed, and weight-related problems, such as teasing, that they encountered in school. They shared strategies for eating more healthy foods and avoiding non-healthy ones. They began to understand the different factors that contributed to their shared obesity. They complained about how hard it was to find clothes that they liked, and they became friends with one another.

Angie's mom and her brother and sister got involved with Angie's efforts to change her behaviors and become healthier, too. They started grocery shopping together and reading labels before putting food in their cart. They wrote down what they ate every day and compared notes after they finished eating dinner. They began monitoring their activity levels and cutting back on their screen time.

Within a couple of months, Angie was finding it was a lot easier to avoid the fast foods she'd eaten in the past, and she actually enjoyed her Tuesday and Thursday afternoon sessions in the school's weight room, where she walked on the treadmill and used a couple of the weight machines. Sure, there were times when she messed up—lots of times, actually, like at her best friend's birthday party when she had a huge piece of cake, or the chocolate-frosted donut she'd eaten at church the other week.

But, as she'd been advised, after those occasions she increased her physical activity and was extra careful about what she ate for a few days. She was watching less TV than she used to and eating a lot of healthy vegetables, and she felt good about herself for the first time in a long time—maybe ever.

As you've read in previous chapters, obesity is a result of energy imbalance. It occurs when energy intake exceeds energy expenditure and energy that is used for growth, causing excessive weight gain. Ultimately, the only way to address and treat obesity is to address this energy imbalance.

The first component of energy imbalance is the number of calories you consume. The second component is the number of calories that you expend, or burn off, plus the calories you use for healthy growth. If you consume more calories than you burn off and use for healthy growth, you gain excessive weight over time. If you consume fewer calories than you burn off or use for healthy growth, you slow down your weight gain or lose weight over time. Sedentary activity, such as watching TV or sitting in front of a computer, also is a factor in energy balance.

Diet, sedentary activity, and physical activity are almost always the first topics addressed in treating obesity. You've probably heard about medicines used in obesity treatment, weight loss surgery, and other options, but modifying diet and activity are the necessary first steps to achieving weight loss. You'll read a little bit about other treatments later in this chapter, but we'll mostly be dealing with issues related to what you eat and your level of physical activity—the two components of energy balance.

Teens and others working toward weight loss often ask whether their goals can be achieved by working only one side of the energy balance equation. Amanda, for instance, might be willing to make some changes to her eating habits, but has no intention of lacing up her sneakers for a 60-minute walk. Justin, on the other hand, is willing to get out on his bike every day and work out a little bit in the weight room, but he's not about to give up his fast-food habit. Amanda and Justin both need to change their thinking: Studies consistently show that those who are successful at weight loss make changes in both their energy intake and expenditure, addressing both diet and physical activity. While it's theoretically possible to lose weight by dramatically reducing the number of calories you eat, or by drastically increasing your physical activity, it's not practical, and it doesn't result in long-term, healthy weight loss.

To understand your own energy balance or imbalance, you need to understand how many calories you take in, and how many you burn off. You read a little bit about tracking calorie intake and expenditure in chapter 2, but in this chapter you'll learn more about counting calories, the nutritional values of some common foods, and how to assess the foods you eat and make some healthy changes.

DETERMINING YOUR DAILY CALORIE GOAL

A calorie, as you read in chapter 2, is a unit of measurement for energy. You need calories for energy to keep your heart beating and your kidneys functioning, to get up, get to school, hang out with friends, do your homework, participate in physical activity, listen to your iPod, and go back to bed. In short, the calories you eat give you energy for life.

It's a little tricky to gauge how many calories you need to eat in a day in order to begin losing some weight. One person who weighs 200 pounds, for instance, might need to eat 2,800 calories a day in order to maintain that weight. Another 200-pound person may need to eat only 2,200 calories a day to stay at the same weight, because that person is spending the entire day in front of the TV while the first is engaging in some physical activity.

If both of those people decide to eat only 1,800 calories a day, the one who needed 2,800 calories in order to maintain his weight will lose weight faster than the person who needed 2,200 calories to remain at a constant weight.

You'll need to experiment a little bit to figure out how many calories you should consume each day in order to lose a pound or two a week. You can make that easier, though, by knowing about how many calories you consumed on the days before you decided to begin making healthy changes and by decreasing that number. If you kept track

To lose one pound a week, you need to consume 500 fewer calories a day than you did when you were maintaining your weight. That's because one pound of body weight equals about 3,500 calories, and there are seven days in a week. If you increase your calorie intake by 500 calories, you'll gain a pound in a week.

of your calorie intake and expenditure for a few days in order to get an idea of your energy balance or imbalance, as was recommended in chapter 2, you might have a pretty good idea of how many calories you need to consume in order to maintain your current weight.

If you can figure out about how many calories you consume each day, you can subtract the number of calories you want to cut, and you'll have your new number. Let's say you were maintaining the same weight by eating 2,500 calories a day. Because a pound equals 3,500 calories, you can lose a pound in a week by consuming 500 fewer calories a day, That means you'd need to consume 2,000 calories a day in order to achieve a one-pound weekly weight loss.

If you increase your activity level and burn more calories, you won't need to cut as many from your food intake. For now, however, let's have a closer look at the calories that are found in different foods.

WHY SOME FOODS ARE BETTER NUTRITIONAL BARGAINS THAN OTHERS

A cup—eight ounces—of skim milk contains about the same number of calories as a cup of regular soda. So, you might think, what's wrong with drinking a glass of soda at lunch instead of a glass of milk?

When you drink a glass of skim milk, which contains about 90 calories, you get considerable amounts of protein, calcium, potassium, and vitamin D, all of which are necessary nutrients. None of those nutrients are present in soda, which contains a large amount of refined sugar. You're getting about the same number of calories, but the soda doesn't provide benefits to your body the way the milk does. Additionally, the skim milk will most likely make you feel more full than the soda, or even than one of these new sugary drinks that contain some proteins and vitamins. If you feel more full, you will unconsciously decrease the amount of calories you eat at that meal or at the next meal, a benefit that the sugary drink will not provide.

Think about this. The serving of french fries—about a cup—that you get in the school cafeteria contains about 250 calories. For the same number of calories, you could eat four and half cups of cooked carrots, which are packed with vitamin A and fiber, and would definitely make you feel full. Because it's not likely that you actually would eat four and a half cups of carrots, consider: If you eat just one cup of carrots—the same serving size as the french fries—you'd consume only 55 calories, compared to the 250 in the fries, and you'd still be getting many, many more times vitamin A and more fiber—a much better nutritional bargain.

Calories that offer little or no nutritional benefit often are referred to as *empty calories,* and the foods and drinks that contain them are not considered to be good nutritional bargains.

Foods that contain a lot of calories—even in small servings—are called *high calorie density foods*. Foods that contain few calories, even in large quantities, are called *low calorie density foods*. High calorie density foods include the following:

> Butter, margarine, mayonnaise, cream-cheese, cream cheese dips, cheese sauce, regular salad dressings
> Nuts and other salty snacks, including potato chips, corn chips, and snack mixes

While some foods are better nutritional bargains than others, some foods also are better calorie bargains than others. For example, a cup of microwave popped, 94-percent-fat-free popcorn contains about 15 calories. A peanut—just one—contains six calories. That means that you can eat four cups of popcorn—a bowlful—and get the same number of calories that you'd get in 10 peanuts—a small handful. That's not to say you should never eat peanuts, or that you should eat popcorn every day, but it points out the caloric differences in different foods. This will become very quickly obvious once you start counting calories!

➤ Bacon and other high-fat meats, including hamburger, steaks, hot dogs, ribs, pepperoni, sausage
➤ Foods fried in fats, including french fries, chicken nuggets, fried chicken or fish
➤ Most cheeses and dishes containing cheese, including macaroni and cheese, vegetable casseroles, pizza, and tacos
➤ Baked goods, cookies, donuts, ice cream, and candy
➤ Sugary drinks such as soda, sweetened ice tea, fruit punch, energy drinks, and sport drinks

The following foods are low calorie density:

➤ Lettuce and other leafy greens
➤ Other vegetables, such as carrots, peas, squash, cucumbers, celery, peppers
➤ Vegetable soups
➤ Lean meats and poultry, such as skinless chicken breast
➤ Broiled fish
➤ Fat-free yogurt, skim milk
➤ Fruits, such as oranges, apples, and berries

You can find a helpful chart listing foods that are low calorie and nutrient dense and those that are calorie dense at We Can!, an online site of the National Institutes of Health. The site is located at www.nhlbi.nih.gov/health/public/heart/obesity/wecan/downloads/go-slow-whoa.pdf. If you want, you could print out the chart and post it on your refrigerator or another handy spot so that you can refer to it when making food choices.

FINDING THE BEST FOODS TO EAT

Trying to figure out what and how much you should be eating can seem complicated and difficult. Once you get the hang of it, however, it won't be so hard. A good resource to start with is MyPyramid, a tool from the U.S. Department of Agriculture that helps you figure out how many servings you should have each day or each week from each food group. It also tells you what constitutes a serving, which may be, for instance, a cup of vegetables.

Generally, MyPyramid recommends a diet rich in whole grains, vegetables, fruits, and low-fat or no-fat dairy products, with reasonable amounts of lean protein, such as beans and meats and poultry with little fat. You can find MyPyramid online at www.mypyramid. gov. The site also contains helpful tools to help you plan menus and

An important distinction to understand is the difference between a portion size and a serving size. A portion is how much of something you would normally eat, while a serving is a standardized amount, often much less than is typically consumed. On the front of a box of a popular breakfast cereal, for example, it says in noticeable print "110 Calories." You might assume, and not unreasonably, that if you fill up your favorite bowl with this cereal, you'll be consuming 110 calories. The cereal you poured into your bowl would be the portion you were going to eat.

Not until you turn the box on its side and read the small print, however, do you learn that one *serving* of cereal contains 110 calories, and that a serving is one cup. One cup of cereal might fill your favorite bowl only halfway, meaning that your usual portion of cereal would have been about 220 calories, compared to one serving at 110 calories. Portion size and serving size can be very different–it's important when you're reading labels and counting calories to pay attention to what constitutes a serving.

formulate a personalized eating plan. It's well worth the time and effort to navigate this site, as there is a lot of good information and advice available.

How the foods you eat are prepared is nearly as important as what is in them. A tuna fish sandwich sounds like a healthy lunch, right? And, with a small can of tuna containing just 150 calories and two slices of thin, whole wheat bread providing about 140 calories and some good nutrients and fiber, it can be a healthy lunch. If you decide to mix two tablespoons of regular mayonnaise (at 100 calories a tablespoon) with the tuna, though, you will have more than doubled the calorie count of the tuna salad. Using light mayonnaise reduces calories added to the tuna by half, as light varieties contain about 50 calories per tablespoon, and fat-free mayonnaise contains only about 10 calories per tablespoon.

Green beans are a healthy vegetable and contain vitamins and fiber, with no fat. You can eat a whole cup of steamed or boiled plain string beans for only 44 calories. Green bean casserole, however—that concoction made with creamy soup, fried onion rings, and

Caloric sweeteners come in many forms other than sugar, and are sometimes overlooked on food labels. Other caloric sweeteners include sucrose, glucose, high-fructose corn syrup, corn syrup, maple syrup, and fructose.

sometimes sour cream, mayonnaise, and cheese that often appears at holiday dinners—can pack on about 150 calories for just half a cup, and contains high amounts of fat and sodium.

You can't control how the food in your school cafeteria is prepared, but you can have a say at how meals are cooked at home. Ask if you can help to prepare dinner, and pay attention to the ingredients that different dishes contain. Use the MyPyramid menu planner and tracker to figure out how many calories are in prepared foods and to help you understand the best methods for preparing foods.

Volunteer to help with food shopping as well, and become a label reader. Check out the number of servings and calories in the foods you're considering taking home. Look to see what the sugar, fat, and sodium contents are, and put the foods that are high in those categories back on the shelf—not in the shopping basket. Food labels inform you of the Percent Daily Value—or % DV—of nutrients contained in the foods we buy. Look for foods that have low % DV of fat, especially saturated fats. Low-fat foods have a % DV of 5 or less, while high-fat foods contain % DVs of 20 or more.

THE COUNT BEGINS

As you begin to think more carefully about what you eat and how to monitor your food intake, you'll learn a lot about the caloric and nutritional contents of different foods. You can learn a lot by reading labels or consulting booklets or Web sites that contain calorie contents. You'll get a handle on what sort of foods contain lots of calories and which are caloric bargains. You'll learn about serving size, get to recognize what servings of different foods look like on a plate or in a bowl, and see how many servings are in the usual portion you eat. You'll practically be an expert in no time!

As you read in chapter 6, it's really important to monitor your behaviors so that you can get a better idea of where you are in terms of energy intake and expenditure. That means recording every single thing you eat and drink, every day, and calculating how many calories you've consumed with a particular food, a particular meal, and on a particular day. You'll also need to record your physical activities in order to understand how much energy you use. You'll read more about that in a little while.

Keeping a record of what you eat doesn't have to be overly complicated, and you don't need to calculate the exact number of calories you consume. If you miss your calorie count by 20 or 30 calories, it's not the end of the world. You do, however, want to be diligent and aware of everything that goes into your mouth. If you gulp down half of a bottle of sports drink without even thinking about it because you're hot and thirsty from cutting the grass, you've consumed calories that need to be recorded. You'll need to be deliberate about recognizing everything you eat and drink, and of keeping track of the amounts that you consume. Until you get used to judging amounts, it's a good idea to measure or weigh what you eat. In time, you'll get to know what a half-cup of peas or a three-ounce serving of meat looks like, and will be able to judge portion sizes without measuring.

There are a number of methods of keeping a food diary. It can be as simple as carrying a small notebook with you in which you keep

Some people fear that their attempts to lose weight may result in eating disorders. They think that keeping a food diary will cause them to obsess over what they eat and result in unhealthy behavior. As stated in chapter 2, however, research has shown that a healthy approach to addressing obesity through changing eating habits and increasing physical activity does not lead to eating disorders. A medically supervised weight loss program, in fact, may even lessen the possibility that eating disorders will occur. If you have decided to start making healthy changes in your eating and physical activity habits, you should feel good about yourself. If you have any concerns about eating disorders, discuss the matter with a parent, the school nurse, your doctor, or another adult.

your records, or you can record and calculate calories and totals using simple software, such as Microsoft Excel, or online tools. MyPyramid offers a feature on which you enter what you've eaten during the day and it calculates not only calories, but nutritional information as well. CalorieKing is another helpful Web site, found at www.calorieking. com. It contains a lot of information, including the calorie and nutritional information for thousands of different foods, and how long you need to do various types of physical activity in order to burn off the calories contained in particular foods.

The important thing about your food diary isn't how you choose to maintain it, but that you are consistent and do it every day and with every food and beverage that you consume. And, remember that it's really important to be completely honest in your food diary, and not try to shave off calories by "forgetting" to record the cupcake you ate at your friend's house that afternoon, or ignoring the pat of butter that you used on the roll you had at dinner or the cheese that was on your sandwich at lunch. The diary is a tool for you to use to get a handle on how many calories you consume. That's all. It's not judgmental, and there's no punishment if the word "cupcake" appears in it. It's strictly meant to help you assess your eating and exercise habits.

Keeping a food diary will quickly teach you about the caloric values of different foods. In time, you'll know that the turkey sandwich you eat two or three days a week contains about 312 calories, and that 220 of those calories are contained in the bread, 66 in the three slices of turkey, and 26 in the half-tablespoon of light mayonnaise you use. You'll remember that you can pile on as much lettuce on that sandwich as you want, because a lettuce leaf contains only about one calorie, and the apple that you eat with the sandwich only adds about 80 calories to your meal.

Keeping track of everything you eat and drink will be difficult sometimes, but it must be done in order to increase your chances of weight loss success.

TRACKING AND INCREASING YOUR PHYSICAL ACTIVITY

While you're keeping track of what you eat, you'll also need to pay attention to the other half of the energy equation—your physical activity. Keeping track of what you do every day allows you to get an idea of how much physical activity you get, and will help you to gauge the energy expenditure side of the energy balance. Just as most of us tend to underestimate how much we eat in a day, most of us tend to overestimate our activity levels. Someone might say, "I run

A reliable pedometer is an excellent tool for helping to monitor your activity level. A pedometer counts and records the number of steps you take each day, helping you to keep track of how much physical activity you're getting. A good brand to look for is Accusplit, which is sold in sporting goods stores or can be ordered online from the company's Web site at www.accusplit.com. Click on "E-Store Online Shopping." The pedometers range in price from about $13 to $30.

around all day long," while, in actuality, she only puts in 4,000 or 5,000 steps.

The U.S. Department of Health and Human Services recommends at least 60 minutes of moderate or vigorous intensity physical activity on most (and preferably all) days for people between the ages of six and 19. Physical activity is beneficial because it burns calories, and it can also help to lower blood pressure and cholesterol, improve your sensitivity to insulin (the hormone that is insufficient in diabetes), help to control appetite, build muscle, and make you feel stronger, improve your self image, and yes, even improve your mood. New research has revealed that regular activity can help to reduce, or even to reverse, the risk factors of heart disease in obese teens.

Hardening of the arteries can begin at an early age in kids with risk factors including obesity and sedentary lifestyles, researchers say. Regular physical activity can reduce the risk of hardening of the arteries and heart disease.

Studies have shown that the great majority of people who not only lose weight but are able to keep it off are those who engage in regular physical activity. Most people who lose weight but do not participate in regular physical activity regain the weight.

All this doesn't mean, however, that you need to jump up and go for an hour-long run or spend an hour every day in the gym.

There are all sorts of ways that you can total an hour's worth of physical activity in a day. It doesn't have to be done all at once, but can be spread out over a day's time. If you walk to school or take the dog for a walk at a brisk pace, that counts as part of your daily activity. Throwing a Frisbee with your friends counts too, along with shoveling snow, mowing the grass, riding your bike, jumping rope, skateboarding, or taking the stairs rather than the elevator or escalator. You should aim for moderate to vigorous activities, some of which are listed below.

Moderate activities:

▸ Brisk walking (about three miles per hour)
▸ Riding a bike (less than 10 miles an hour)
▸ Hiking
▸ Gardening or yard work
▸ Dancing
▸ Playing tennis doubles
▸ Jumping on a trampoline
▸ In-line skating at a moderate pace or skateboarding
▸ Playing table tennis
▸ Yoga

Vigorous activities:

▸ Playing competitive sports such as soccer, basketball, or field hockey
▸ Running or jogging (five miles per hour)
▸ Riding a bike (more than 10 miles per hour)
▸ Swimming laps
▸ Very fast walking (more than four miles per hour)
▸ Aerobics
▸ Playing tennis singles
▸ Karate or judo
▸ Circuit weight training
▸ Vigorous in-line skating

An important point to keep in mind is that you can increase the number of calories you burn off just by making very simple changes. Standing burns off more calories than sitting. Running up the steps uses more calories than walking. You can increase the number of calories you expend by jumping around or dancing while you're watching TV, or by doing some leg lifts while you talk on the phone.

And remember that the level of intensity at which you exercise changes how effective it is and how many calories you'll expend. Running, for instance, requires more calories than jogging. Leisurely pedaling your bike or stationary bike requires a lower calorie expenditure than biking as fast as you can.

If you've been sedentary in the past, meaning that you've engaged in no or very little physical activity, you shouldn't try to begin with an hour. If you determine you've been physically active for only 10 minutes a day, try to increase your daily activity to 20 minutes, and maintain that level for two weeks. One you're used to 20 minutes a day, increase your activity time to 30 minutes and continue with that for another two weeks. Keep on increasing your time by 10 minutes until you hit the recommended hour's worth of activity. If you've been very inactive for a period of time, you should check with a doctor before you begin with an activity program.

You can make your own exercise diary, or download a good one from the Internet. Just make sure that for each entry you include the date, the activity, how long you performed the activity, and the level at which you performed it. If you want to, you can make a note describing your mood before you began the activity and when you finished, and keep a record of your heart rate during the activity. You can download and print a simple, effective food and activity chart at www.nhlbi.nih.gov/health/public/heart/obesity/lose_wt/diary.ndf.

Just as with keeping a food diary, keeping a physical activity diary isn't meant to put you on a guilt trip. If you aren't physically active for a day or two because you didn't have time, or you didn't feel well, or you just couldn't gather up the energy to get moving, it's not the end of the world. The point of the diary is to give you a better idea of how much physical activity you're getting, and how it might be affecting your efforts at losing weight.

TRACKING AND DECREASING SEDENTARY ACTIVITY

While it's important to get a handle on your activity level and to work to increase it, it's also important to figure out how much sedentary activity you engage in, and to work on decreasing that time.

Getting an hour of exercise each day is great, but if the rest of the time you are sitting and watching TV, that is not so great. Sedentary activity

Your job, as you work to make healthy lifestyle changes, has three parts. You'll need to monitor and record your eating and drinking, your physical activity level, and your sedentary activity level. Do not attempt, however, to begin monitoring all three at the same time. It doesn't matter so much which order you choose, but begin by tracking one of those three items. So, if you choose to start monitoring and recording what you eat and drink, do only that for four to six weeks until you're used to it and it's not a big deal anymore. At that point, you can begin tracking and recording either your physical or sedentary activity, adding that to your nutrition tracking. Once you've done that for a few weeks, add the third component to really help you to get a handle on your energy balance.

includes watching TV or DVDs, playing video games, surfing the Internet, chatting online, texting, or talking on the phone. The problem with sedentary activity is that it detracts from your opportunities for physical activity. If you're sitting in your room playing a video game, you're not out riding your bike or shooting hoops with some friends.

Monitor how much sedentary activity you do, and then work to decrease that amount of time. Behavioral research has demonstrated that it is more effective for weight loss to focus on decreasing sedentary activity than to focus on increasing physical activity, so it's really important that you're aware of your sedentary activity and try to minimize it.

You can do this the same way you track calorie intake and physical activity, by being aware of what you do and keeping a record of it.

After you have an idea of how much time you spend on sedentary activity, work on decreasing that time. For instance, if you have five hours of sedentary activities in a typical day, try to cut one hour of sedentary activity each day for the next two weeks.

So, instead of going right to your room to watch TV after you finish eating dinner, try to keep the TV turned off until the show that you really want to see comes on. At the end of the two weeks, cut another hour. You also can turn sedentary activity into physical activity using a Wii or another interactive gaming system instead of the type where you simply sit and play.

OTHER TREATMENTS FOR OBESITY

Dietary changes, decrease in sedentary activities, and increased physical activity are the cornerstones of obesity treatment. Most experts agree that these should be the first things done to manage obesity. While some teens are able to use information such as that contained in this book to make healthy changes on their own, others may need professional help. If you have tried many times to make healthy changes on your own and have not been successful, you might need to seek help from a doctor who specializes in obesity issues, or who at least is well versed on the problem.

Weight loss centers are available in many areas, often in conjunction with universities at which obesity research is under way. These centers usually offer professional services such as diet, behavioral, and exercise counseling, along with medical care from physicians or nurse practitioners.

Check the appendix in the back of this book for more information about finding professional help, or discuss your concerns with your doctor. You'll learn more about the cost of care, what services generally are covered by insurance, and how to get care if you can't afford to pay for it in the last chapter of this book.

MEDICATIONS

In some cases, a doctor may prescribe medication to help with weight loss. Two weight loss medications that have been approved for adolescents and teens are *sibutramine* (Meridia) and *orlistat* (Allī). Sibutramine is one of a class of medications called appetite suppressants, which means they act on appetite control centers in the brain to make you feel less hungry. Orlistat is in a class of drugs called lipase inhibitors. These work in the intestines by blocking the digestion of some fats.

An important thing to understand is that weight loss medications are prescribed in *addition* to dietary and lifestyle changes, not in *place* of. And, as with any medication, sibutramine and orlistat contain potential side effects, some of which can be serious.

WEIGHT CONTROL SURGERY

Obesity surgery, called bariatric surgery, is becoming more common among adolescents and teens. Between 2000 and 2003, the number of surgeries on youth between the ages of 12 and 19 tripled, with 771 surgeries performed in 2003. In contrast, 104,702 adults underwent bariatric surgery in 2003. It is generally agreed that weight control surgery in teens is a last resort, to be used only in dire situations where the health consequences of obesity are thought to be more serious than the consequence of the surgery.

The most common forms of weight loss surgery are gastric bypass and *gastric banding*. In gastric bypass surgery, which is the most commonly used procedure, a small pouch is created at the top of the stomach, and the rest of the stomach is sealed off. The pouch is connected directly to the second section of the small intestine, meaning that food bypasses the stomach and the first section of the small intestine, and that only small amounts of food can be consumed.

Gastric banding is the process of placing a silicone band around the upper part of the stomach, which creates a pouch and reduces the amount of food the stomach can hold. Gastric banding does not change the anatomy of the digestive system, as gastric bypass surgery does; it merely restricts the amount of food the stomach can hold. There is more than one type of gastric banding, but the most common is laparoscopic adjustable gastric banding, often called lap banding.

Weight loss surgery for teens is controversial. Extensive medical and psychological evaluations are necessary prior to surgery, and nutritional problems may occur following surgery. In addition, some teens who have undergone bariatric surgery have reported emotional and psychological problems.

WHAT YOU NEED TO KNOW

➤ What and how much you eat, how much time you spend in sedentary activities, and your level of physical activity are the first considerations in the treatment of obesity.

➤ To determine how many calories you should consume in order to lose weight, you need to know how many calories it takes for you to maintain your current weight.

➤ High calorie density foods, such as deep-fried chicken or cookies, are those that contain a lot of calories even in small amounts. Low calorie density foods, such as vegetables or fruits, contain relatively few calories even in large amounts.

➤ Keeping track of what you eat and drink, your physical activity, and your sedentary activity is critical to help you in your efforts to lose weight.

➤ Other treatments for obesity include specialized medical care, medications, and weight loss surgery.

8

A Long-Term Approach for Achieving and Maintaining Healthy Weight

While losing weight can be difficult, maintaining weight loss is even harder. It is, however, possible if you're willing to commit to a lifelong approach. It stands to reason that, if you reach a weight that's desirable for you and then revert to old habits, like stopping by the fast-food restaurant after school for a cheeseburger and french fries before you head home to play video games, you're not going to maintain your weight loss. In fact, you could end up even heavier than you were before you made your lifestyle changes. So it is really important to think about maintenance of weight loss, plan for it, and to make sure that you are committed to long-term changes from the start, before even starting any weight loss program. If you're not willing to make a long-term commitment, it's not worth the effort.

It's an unfortunate fact that many people lose significant amounts of weight only to regain it in a relatively short time. Others, however, are successful at maintaining weight loss, and that has generated a lot of interest among researchers who are working to find out how they do it.

The good news is that research shows that people who are able to maintain weight loss for between two and five years (they are called "successful losers"!) increase their odds of achieving permanent weight loss. And, since the basic principles of keeping weight off are the same as those used to lose weight, you already have an idea of how it works. In this chapter, we'll look at some practical methods for maintaining a healthy weight, and a healthy and happy lifestyle overall.

Let's consider some of the things you'll want to do to stay on track with your weight loss. You might be surprised to find out how many of these strategies you're already familiar with.

KEEP YOUR EYE ON THE PRIZE OF GOOD HEALTH

If you weren't concerned about being healthy, you probably wouldn't be reading this book. If you've already taken steps toward changing behaviors in order to lose weight, hopefully you've done so out of regard for your health, and in hopes of achieving other benefits such as improved self-esteem that often occur with weight loss. If you've lost some weight by now—even a small amount— you've taken an important step in assuring you'll be as healthy as possible.

If your health is the reason that you decided you wanted to lose weight, it should be an equally important reason for maintaining weight loss. Focusing on being healthy is a positive action that can help you to make the right choices regarding nutrition and activity. Having the lifestyle of a healthy person is something good that you can do for yourself.

Sure, there will be occasions when it's really difficult to make good food and activity choices, and there will be days when you'll encounter setbacks. Even on those days, however, you should continue to look forward and keep health the focus of your efforts.

Take a few minutes to think about why you decided to take charge of your health in the first place. Maybe you were tired of being out of breath when you climbed the stairs at school, or worried that somebody would make fun of you because of your weight. Maybe you just felt ready to make a change.

If you've lost some weight by this point, try to compare how you feel now to how you felt before you began your weight loss program. What's better about your new weight and your new, healthier lifestyle?

Losing weight will help you to be healthier in the future. Even if you lose only a few pounds, you've taken an important step by preventing yourself from gaining any more weight. Many people gain weight over time. If you only manage to keep your weight steady, you're better off than if you continued to gain weight.

CONTINUE TO SELF-MONITOR YOUR BEHAVIORS

You've learned that it's extremely important while trying to lose weight to monitor your behaviors regarding what and how much you eat, your physical activity, and your sedentary activity. Self-monitoring is also critical in your chances for long-term success in keeping weight off.

Most of us have a tendency to let things slide now and then. You might figure it won't hurt to skip your walk for a couple of days, or to have a big piece of apple pie with ice cream for dessert. And, if you did those things only very, very occasionally, it wouldn't hurt. Unfortunately, little slides can become habits in just a little bit of time, before you even realize what's happening.

As noted in previous chapters, most of us are very bad at assessing how much we eat and how much physical activity we get. We tend to think we eat less than we do and are more physically active than we really are. We're also not very good at judging portion sizes, and when we stop monitoring our portions they tend to get bigger and bigger.

By the time you notice, you could be eating much more food than you need to satisfy your hunger and maintain energy balance and keep the weight off.

By continuing to self-monitor, however, you're forced to confront what you've eaten and how much physical and sedentary behavior you've done. Little "slides" can be recognized and dealt with before they have a chance to become habitual.

Self-monitoring includes keeping track of your weight, which leads to the question of how often you should weigh yourself. Some people like to weigh themselves every day, but others find that to be discouraging because of weight fluctuations that are beyond their control, such as fluid shifts. Getting on the scale once a week is generally recommended, and is a good way for most people to gauge their progress and weight loss maintenance. Remember to keep a record of your weight so you can continue to track it.

Ideally, tracking your nutrition and activity levels will become something that you do nearly without even thinking about it.

EAT ON A REGULAR SCHEDULE AND STOP WHEN YOU'VE HAD ENOUGH

We all have probably had the experience of eating way more than we were really hungry for, and feeling uncomfortably full afterward. It's easy to eat more than you need, even more than you want, if you're not paying attention. This results in the condition called "mindless eating," which you've encountered in earlier chapters of this book. Self-monitoring will help you to avoid mindless eating and keep your portion sizes under control. Eating at regular times instead of just grabbing something whenever you feel hungry is very important in avoiding overeating. Be intentional about your meals, making sure they are planned, and avoid eating between meals, unless it's a snack that is in your plan. Some other tips to avoid mindless eating are:

▶ Measure or weigh the foods you eat.
▶ Put only a predetermined amount of food on your plate.
▶ Use smaller plates and cups.
▶ Put food away after getting the portion you want to eat.
▶ Don't finish all the food on your plate.
▶ Don't do anything else (read, watch TV, etc.) while you eat.

If you notice an upward trend while tracking your weight, increase your self-monitoring of food intake, physical activity, and sedentary activity, and try to determine how your energy intake and expenditure has become unbalanced. Before you gain any more weight, adjust your food intake or your activity level—or perhaps both—so that you're taking in fewer calories, burning off more calories, or both. Paying attention and taking action when you gain a little bit of weight will provide better results than waiting until you've gained a lot of weight and feeling like you're starting from scratch.

> Concentrate on what you are eating, and take time to enjoy each bite.

> Put your fork down between bites of food so your body has time to let you know it's getting full.

> Don't wait until you're feeling starved to eat. If you feel very hungry between your scheduled meals, try a low calorie density snack, such as fruit, which should keep you feeling satisfied until your next meal.

> If you're bored and thinking about eating for something to do, call a friend, take a walk, or engage in some other activity.

> When you're at home, eat only at the kitchen or dining room table.

> When eating out, order the smallest portions you can and avoid the temptation to add to or "supersize" your order.

EAT A VARIETY OF FOODS THAT YOU LIKE

Now and then a particular "diet" will attract a lot of attention. The grapefruit diet. The cabbage soup diet. The low-carb diet. The cereal diet. The smoothie meal-replacement diet. These diets usually require that you eat a lot of a few particular foods and very little of other foods. The problem is, once you're so tired of eating cabbage soup that you can't bear to think about another bowl, you're likely to be feeling deprived and ready to chuck it all and head out in search of a double cheeseburger.

No one food can provide all the nutrients you need or keep you satisfied with what you're eating. It's important to eat a variety of foods that you like in order to stay healthy and feel content. Hopefully, you've already become familiar with MyPyramid, the government Web site that explains food groups and nutrients found within them, number of recommended daily servings, portion size, and other topics. If not, be sure to check it out at www. mypyramid.gov.

Some people limit their food choices because they claim not to like vegetables or fruits, or they refuse to eat any dairy products or fish. While sometimes there is good reason for avoiding certain foods, such as in the case of food allergies, often people refuse to eat a certain food or foods simply because they've never tried it, or because they've had a bad experience with that particular food. Willingness to try new foods or foods you may not have liked in the past is likely to result in some pleasant discoveries and a greater variety of foods for you to eat.

KEEP UP YOUR PHYSICAL ACTIVITY AND KEEP DOWN YOUR SEDENTARY ACTIVITY

Just as physical activity is a key component in losing weight, it's also key to maintaining weight loss and staying fit. Remember that there are many benefits to physical activity, including strong bones and muscles, a healthy body, increased energy, improved mood, stress relief, increased strength and endurance, improved sleep, and improved mental health. Physical activity is a vital part of a healthy lifestyle.

Choosing activities that you enjoy will help assure that you continue to participate. If running is a drag for you, try swimming or biking instead. If there are no recreational facilities available where you live, check out the school gym or a community activity program. Many people find it easier to maintain a high level of physical activity when they engage a friend or family member and do it together.

And, remember that you can incorporate physical activity into your regular day if you're intentional about it. When possible, walk or bike instead of driving or getting a ride, do sit-ups during commercials when you watch TV, and run up the steps in the mall instead of using the escalator. Chores such as washing and waxing the car, raking leaves, and shoveling snow also are good ways of maintaining physical activity and burning calories. And they'll make your parents happy too.

As you're paying attention to physical activity, remember the flip side—sedentary activity, and be mindful about minimizing it when possible. If you still have a TV in your bedroom, move it out. Studies show that kids who have TVs in their bedrooms watch one and half hours more TV a day than those who don't. Limit your screen time—including TV, video games, and computer use (other than for homework)—to two hours or less per day, substituting activities that get you moving instead.

LEARN TO RECOGNIZE AND DEAL WITH EMOTIONAL EATING AND INACTIVITY

Many people, perhaps including you, use food or inactivity to deal with negative emotions like sadness, anger, nervousness, or frustration, or to respond to a stressful or difficult situation. Have you ever been in a situation where something goes wrong and your response is to grab a box of cookies or lie in front of the TV (or both) in order to avoid thinking about how you feel or to make yourself feel better?

Maybe you have a fight with a friend or a parent, or your cell phone gets stolen during gym class, or somebody says something that makes you feel really bad. Instead of dealing with the problem, you try to comfort yourself with food or avoid thinking about it by watching TV. You might not even realize what you're doing, or at least why you're doing it.

While the cookies and TV might provide a quick fix, you're likely to end up feeling worse than ever once you acknowledge what has happened. You might feel like you've ruined everything, and that your previous efforts to lose weight don't matter.

The truth is, however, that lapses are a normal part of behavior change, and while it's important to try to prevent them from happening, it's equally important to know how to bounce back from them when they do occur. None of us can completely avoid unpleasant or stressful situations—they are part of living. We can, however, develop coping strategies, such as the ones described below, to help us deal with them in a healthy manner, without resorting to a box of cookies or three hours in front of the TV.

- ▸ Identify triggers that may result in overeating or inactivity and think about how you might avoid or reverse them. If you hate more than anything to fight with your best friend, but you've been upset with her for three days because she didn't include you when she went to the mall and you definitely feel a fight coming on, talk to her about the situation in order to get the problem into the open before you end up having the fight. Keeping your cell phone locked up during gym class will minimize the chances of it being stolen and you thrown into a stressful situation.
- ▸ Plan ahead how you can minimize the magnitude of a setback. There will be days—like when you know you're going to get the test back that you already know you failed—when you're just going to need Ben & Jerry's Chocolate Fudge Brownie ice cream. There's no avoiding it. All you're going to want to do is head home, grab that 1,000-calorie pint out of the freezer, find a spoon, and console yourself. How about, though, stopping instead at the convenience store on your way home and buying the 3.6 ounce, 240-calorie mini-cup of the same brand and flavor, and eating it slowly? The ice cream will taste just as good, but you will have limited the "damage." Planning before the emotion occurs makes it more likely that you'll be able to make thoughtful decisions, rather than those that are driven by how bad you feel.

> ➤ Give yourself time and space to deal with a problem. Ignoring a problem doesn't make the problem disappear, and the problem may even intensify. Sometimes it's important to put other activities aside in order to be able to devote your attention to a problem or stressor.
> ➤ Seek support from someone who can help you deal with problems or stressful situations, especially if the situation is serious. Find a friend who will listen to you rant about the teacher who gave you that test you failed, or the loser who stole your cell phone. If you have a serious issue, such as you're being bullied in school or living with an unpleasant situation at home, identify an adult with whom you can talk.
> ➤ Look for a sense of perspective regarding your problem or stressor. Usually a difficult situation is just that—a difficult situation, but not the end of the world. Some events, such as the death of a loved one or divorce of parents, are life-altering, and will take time and perhaps even professional help to recover from. A fight with your best friend, however, is a passing situation that you probably won't even remember in a couple of weeks.

There will be days when you slip up and eat way more than you should, or end up lying around watching movies for five hours. Slip-ups here and there are to be expected, and, as you just read, you can employ coping strategies to help you deal with and recover from them.

What happens, though, if a slip up lasts for weeks rather than a day? How do you prepare for a situation such as visiting your grandmother (who loves to cook all your favorite foods) for three weeks during the summer, or going away to camp for two weeks, during which time you'll have no control over the food that's served?

Just as you can plan for a one-time slipup on a given day, you can plan on how you'll deal with a longer period of difficulty in staying on your healthy eating and activity program.

A good way to start is to learn to anticipate periods of time in which it will be difficult for you to maintain healthy eating and activity habits. If your grandmother has served you cakes and pies after each meal every other time that you've visited her, chances are good that she's going to do so again. Knowing that, however, gives you an advantage.

Just as with a short-term situation, such as eating to help you cope with a bad grade on your math test, you can plan ahead for how you can minimize the "damage" from your visit to Grandma's house.

First of all, you can explain to Grandma, or ask your parent to explain to her, that you have been working hard to maintain healthy eating and activity patterns, and would be better off without a constant supply of cake and pie and other unhealthy foods. If you suspect that Grandma will go ahead and bake for you anyway, think about how you might increase your physical activity level and decrease sedentary activity.

If you're at camp and have no control over the foods offered, remember what you've learned about nutrition and make choices that are as healthy as possible. Look for fresh fruit and vegetables. Choose cereal rather than sausage and eggs for breakfast, and ask if nonfat milk is available.

As much as you may want to keep practicing healthy behavior changes, it's possible that you might "fall off the wagon" for an extended period of time. If it turns out that you return from Grandma's house, having eaten pie, cake, donuts, and every other baked good imaginable every day for three weeks, it's not the end of the world.

The first thing to understand is that your original decision and efforts to make healthy behavior changes have not been wasted. Even if you reverted back to unhealthy habits for a month, you can get back on track and reestablish the healthy behaviors that you had set into place. You're not starting over; you're merely picking up where you left off.

Think about the techniques you used when you first started your weight loss program, and reemploy them now. Self-monitoring your food intake, physical activity level, and sedentary activity will be critical. Count your calories and increase your physical activity. If you feel that it's too difficult to maintain healthy eating and activity levels on your own, talk to your parent about joining a support group or enrolling in a specialized program. That may help get you back on track after a period that makes you feel really lousy because you didn't live up to the commitments that you made to yourself. Then again, remember that everybody has setbacks and the key is how you deal with the situation when it happens.

Whatever you do, don't give up. Making the initial decision to change behaviors in order to improve your health was a huge step, and you owe it to yourself to carry through with that decision. Losing weight is not an easy undertaking, and, once you've lost some weight, there are challenges in keeping it off. Because your weight can affect your health, however, it's important that you pay attention and work to keep it under control. Keeping a positive attitude and remembering that good health is your goal isn't always easy, but will help you to navigate the struggles of weight loss and bounce back when setbacks occur.

WHAT YOU NEED TO KNOW

> Losing weight is difficult, and keeping it off is even more of a challenge. There are strategies you can use, however, to minimize the risk of gaining the weight back and, instead, to continue with a healthy lifestyle.

> Continuing to self-monitor your behaviors regarding eating and activity will help you keep track of your progress and to avoid slipups that can, if repeatedly ignored, become habits.

> Being aware of how much you eat and where, how, and when you eat will help you to avoid the common practice of "mindless eating."

> Finding physical activities that are enjoyable will help assure that you remain involved and active. Activity also can be incorporated into your everyday routine.

> It's easy to eat because you're angry or upset or bored, or for another negative reason. Learning how to recognize and deal with emotional eating can lead to fewer episodes and help you to handle them better when they do occur.

> Even a longer lapse period doesn't mean that you can't pick up where you left off and resume your efforts to practice healthy behaviors that will lead to weight loss and weight maintenance.

9

Strategies for Dealing with Obesity in Daily Life

No doctor is going to tell you that it's good for you to be obese. What more and more doctors are recognizing, however, is that those who are obese experience obesity every day, and also that they may be able to achieve significant benefits to their health and quality of life with small doable changes. Some health professionals also understand better that they must work toward helping obese patients be as healthy and happy as possible on a daily basis, rather than focusing on weight loss alone.

In this chapter, we'll address a range of issues that affect obese teens, including healthy living, activities of daily living, body image, dating, and so forth. Although teens are often able to adjust to and compensate for difficulties in these areas better than adults, as you know, problems do arise from time to time. Thinking in advance how you might handle certain situations can help to prepare you in the event that they occur.

TUNING IN TO YOUR HEALTH

You've read quite a bit already in this book about health issues that are associated with obesity, including diabetes, sleep disorders, high blood pressure, breathing problems, and even some adult cancers. Because you've made a decision to take control and work at lifestyle changes that will improve your overall health, you can avoid, or at least delay, these serious conditions. As an obese teenager, however, you are more at risk for health problems than are people your age who aren't obese.

Because of that, it's extremely important for you to be aware of your body, of how you feel, and to recognize warning signs of trouble.

A disturbing fact is that people who are obese tend to delay or put off health care altogether. This can be caused by embarrassment at being weighed, fear that health care providers will admonish the patient or offer unsolicited advice regarding weight, or even discomfort at not fitting comfortably into a gown or onto an examination table. This delay pertains to both preventative care, such as blood pressure, gynecologic, or diabetes screenings, as well as optimal care for existing conditions.

If you haven't had a physical exam for a long time, like more than a year, you should talk to your parent about making sure you get one. Having a physical accomplishes several things: It allows a doctor to determine if you have any present conditions, such as high cholesterol or blood pressure that you would not notice on your own, and it establishes a baseline, so that your doctor can tell if your physical health is changing in the future.

It is also important to establish a comfortable and trustful relationship with a primary care provider so that when something comes up, you have someone you already know and trust to turn to. If you feel that your doctor is judging you or is disrespectful because of your obesity, don't hesitate to find another doctor. You need to have a trustful partner in your health care who you respect and who respects you. Adolescence and young adulthood can be particularly challenging times in which to build a long-term partnership with a health care provider. These are the years when patients often shift their care over from a pediatrician to an adult-care physician. For those who go away to college, it may be difficult to figure out if it's better to see someone close to home or close to the school. In making these choices, try to remember that trust, respect, and long-term partnership with a medical professional will be key to your health.

Because conditions such as type 2 diabetes are becoming increasingly common in teens, it's important to be aware of symptoms. Take a few minutes to review chapter 5, which includes symptoms of illnesses associated with obesity. If you notice any changes in your health, or anything that just doesn't seem right, don't hesitate to tell a parent or other adult about it. Pay attention to your body so that you're aware of changes or problems. Remember though, that some conditions, including high blood pressure, elevated cholesterol and triglycerides, hardening of the arteries, insulin resistance, metabolic syndrome, fatty liver, and left heart ventricular hypertrophy, have no or few symptoms, meaning that you will not be aware of them unless your physician looks for them with special tests.

PERSONAL CARE

Personal care can be something of a challenge for obese people, but there are many techniques and assistive equipment to help. Obesity can result in limited range of motion, making it difficult for some people to perform tasks such as washing or wiping themselves after toileting, or bending over to clip toenails. It might seem embarrassing to talk about, but it's important to maintain good hygiene for your health and so that you feel self-assured and confident. If you are having problems with keeping yourself clean or performing other personal care tasks, you might feel like you can't discuss it with anyone, or that you're the only person experiencing these sorts of difficulties. The truth is that a lot of people are having the same sorts of problems, and people have been working hard to come up with ways to address and solve those problems. As a result, there are a whole range of *assistive devices* you can get to help with personal care and the activities of daily living.

> ➤ Sammons Preston Rehab Equipment & Supplies (www.sammons preston.com) offers a wide range of aids to daily living as well as health-care equipment.
> ➤ Dynamic Living (www.dynamic-living.com) is a Web site offering many products especially designed to assist with personal hygiene.
> ➤ Living XL (www.livingxl.com) has a variety of products intended for overweight and obese customers. It also offers personal care products such as lotion applicators, blood pressure monitors with larger cuffs, and larger bath towels.
> ➤ Allegro Medical Supplies (www.allegromedical.com) makes it easy to find what you need because you can shop by condition. Allegro offers an extensive variety of assistive devices.

If you have a hard time figuring out how to accomplish your personal care or other activities of daily living more easily, consider getting help from a professional. This is what *occupational therapists* do for a living, and your insurance may be willing to cover such consultation. Occupational therapists frequently work with people recovering from a disease or an accident, elderly people, or those with chronic conditions that make simple daily activities difficult. They are well aware, therefore, of tools available that help compensate for the physical limitations that some obese people experience.

Staying clean is key to good personal hygiene, which means frequent showering or baths. Using deodorant systematically is a good idea, making sure it contains an antiperspirant if you're prone to perspiring. Don't try to mask body odor with perfumes, powders, or body sprays—that generally just makes the situation worse.

Skin fold irritation and infection is a common source of concern among people who are obese. The best thing you can do to avoid these problems is to make sure you dry thoroughly after bathing. Some people use a hair dryer to make sure their skin is completely dry. Medicated powder dusted into skin folds can help to absorb moisture. If infection occurs in skin folds, you may need to apply a topical antifungal agent or medicated cream. Talk to a health care provider if infection becomes a problem.

If you are bothered by friction irritation caused when one area of skin rubs against another (usually in the thighs), consider wearing a layer of spandex to protect the skin. You also can find some good creams, such as PuraCare Active Sports Cream or Bodyglide Anti-Chafe skin protection stick that are formulated to prevent chafing from skin friction. If you can't find these products in a store, check online or go to a bike shop in your area, as these products are very popular with long-distance bikers.

Remember that most teenagers are self-conscious about their bodies, regardless of how big or small they are. It's practically a rite of passage as a teen to worry about how you look—if your hair is too greasy, if you might have body odor, if you have too many pimples, and so on. The best you can do is to keep yourself clean and neatly groomed and to try not to be overly self-conscious.

OTHER ACTIVITIES OF DAILY LIVING

Just as there are aids and techniques to make personal care more manageable, there are things you can do to make activities of daily living, such as getting dressed or simply getting around, easier to accomplish.

For example, if you experience the common problem of difficulty tying your shoes, there are a couple of things you can do. One is to buy elastic shoelaces, which you simply pull to tighten. If you have trouble bending over to tie your shoes or become winded when you do, try sitting on the floor with your back against a wall or cross one foot over the opposite knee. It's really a trial-and-error process to find out what works best for you. You've probably already found lots of useful strategies to minimize the impact of weight on your daily living.

There also are devices available from the companies listed above to help you pull on socks, grabbers that help you reach objects without having to bend over, long-handled shoehorns, and many others.

Seating is often a source of concern and embarrassment. Many seats in school buses, movie theaters, amusement park rides, airplanes, and even cars clearly were not designed with obese people in mind. If you're faced with this problem, look for seats that don't have arms. Bench seats are more accommodating than individual ones. As the incidence of obesity increases, we're starting to see some larger seating options available, as on amusement park rides. There is, however, a long way to go in resolving this issue and usually, as an individual, you can't do much to change things. However, as we've discussed in other chapters, you can team up with others to advocate for a more friendly environment for you and others who live with obesity.

Another issue for many obese teenagers is their sleeping patterns. Many teens come home from school and take a nap. While most everyone could benefit from an occasional afternoon nap, making it habitual isn't a good idea for a couple of reasons.

If you're napping after school, what aren't you doing? Napping isn't a social activity, and isolation among obese teens already tends to be an issue. Coming home to sleep after school only increases that isolation.

Another problem is that napping after school tends to make you less tired at what would be an ideal bedtime. As a result, many teens stay up very late at night and don't get as much sleep as they need to in order to feel well-rested in the morning. This leads to a cycle of feeling tired during the school day, coming home and taking a nap, staying up late because you're not tired at night, and so on.

If you're an afternoon napper, try to give up your snooze time and head to bed earlier at night. It will take a little while for your system to get used to the changes, but chances are you'll start feeling more rested and generally better.

Being physically active also contributes to an overall sense of wellness. It's important to remember that physical activity is not restricted to organized sports or working out in a gym. Many of your daily activities contribute to the physical activity you get. Pushing the lawn mower, walking up and down steps, dashing out to the mailbox, or even strolling through the aisles of the grocery store (except the junk food aisle!) all count as physical activity. The more active you are in the course of your normal day, and the less inactive you are (for example by consciously limiting the amount of television you are watching), the more physical activity you'll accomplish.

If you enjoy sports and think you'd like to participate in an organized sports activity, give it a try. Not every sport involves running up and down a field or around a track for hours on end. In fact, in many sports, being overweight is not a disadvantage, and may even be an advantage. You might be a good football player or a wrestler. Maybe you will enjoy ice hockey or water polo, or swimming, field hockey, shot put or discus throwing, bicycling—whatever. In addition to the health benefits, being involved in a sport makes you part of a team, which brings about a sense of belonging and makes you less likely to be teased or picked on.

If you give it a try and find that the particular position in the sport you've chosen is too difficult, talk to your coach about switching to a different position or finding something else to do for the team. You can even look into being an equipment manager, or ask if you can help the athletic trainer. You'd still be involved and part of the team, even if you weren't participating as an athlete, and for sure will get more physical activity than if you just sit in front of the TV.

Another option is to join an intramural sport, which tends to be less competitive and intense. Or, look for a community recreation program, such as a volleyball or a bowling league. If you really want to participate in a sporting event but don't feel capable of keeping up, think about a sports program for kids who have disabilities, such as the Special Olympics. Many teens report positive experiences from these sorts of activities.

FASHION AND SHOPPING

A frequent complaint among people who are overweight or obese is that they have trouble finding fashionable clothing that fits them. Fortunately, this situation has improved and continues to improve as designers and manufacturers move to meet the needs of a population with increasing diversity in body size.

And, while many teens enjoy shopping at the mall or in other stores, if you don't, there now are many online shopping locations where you can buy clothes. Sites like Casual Male XL, found at www.casualmale.com, offers brand-named clothing including Nautica, Polo, and Levi's; shirts, sweatshirts, and other items bearing professional and college sports logos; and urban-style clothing. Waist sizes are available up to 60 inches and sizes go to 8X. Casual Male also has walk-in stores, for which locations are given online. Other places that offer fashionable clothing in plus sizes include the following:

> ➤ Torrid at www.torrid.com. Cutting-edge women's clothing in sizes 12 to 26.
> ➤ Alight.com at www.alight.com. Fashionable, trendy clothing for teens and women in sizes 14 to 30.

Living XL is geared entirely toward making life more comfortable for plus-sized customers. The company, online at www.livingXL.com, offers products ranging from patio furniture to car and airplane seat belt extenders. A sampling of products includes scales that accommodate up to 1,000 pounds, a heavy-duty camp cot, travel belts in sizes up to 72, durable hammocks, a full line of clothing, and much more.

> ▸ Just My Size at www.jms.com. Brand-name women's underwear, lingerie and swimsuits in sizes 14 to 40, with bra sizes from 38A to 58J.
> ▸ Big and Tall Guys at www.bigandtallguys.com. Jeans to formalwear with waist sizes to 60 and shirts, underwear, athletic wear, and other clothing in sizes up to 8X.
> ▸ Old Navy Women's Plus at www.oldnavy.com. A variety of clothing in sizes 16 to 30, available online only.
> ▸ Living XL at www.livingXL.com. Clothing for men in sizes up to 6X and women up to 4X.

Walk-in stores also are starting to feature more clothing in larger sizes. Target and Wal-Mart offer plus sizes for men, women, and juniors. Torrid has walk-in locations, primarily in California, and many other stores offer larger sizes in order to attract and satisfy customers.

As demand for stylish clothing in larger sizes increases, overweight and obese teens will have more and more choices. Have fun, be creative, and create your own look. One teen reported that she wasn't satisfied with the plus-sized clothing that she claimed "looked like something my grandmother would wear," so she moved to the men's department and bought polo shirts, T-shirts, and shorts.

RELATIONSHIPS

Relationships and dating are important to most teens and, while sometimes wonderful, teen relationships also can be stressful and disappointing. Obese teens often feel left out of the dating scene, despite being open to the possibilities of dating. Despite high and increasing rates of obesity, the same stigma that obese people experience in jobs, health care, and education also extends to romantic relationships.

A study conducted in 2005 at the University of Washington asked 449 college students to identify with whom they would most prefer or least prefer to engage in an intimate relationship. Both males and females said they would least prefer a relationship with someone who was obese, even more so than someone who was physically handicapped or experiencing mental illness.

While that is discouraging news, both to those who are obese and all who are concerned with the stigma that obese people face, it does not mean that you will never date or find happy, lasting relationships. Indeed, you may already be dating or in a relationship. If not, you have something in common with lots and lots of teenagers who find it more comfortable to hang out with groups of friends instead of being one-on-one with a romantic partner.

The teen years often are portrayed as a time of frequent dating, experimenting with relationships, and improving social skills. Don't

Sometimes, even though it seems scary, you need to put yourself out there and take the initiative to ask someone for a date. If you don't, you could end up missing out on a great relationship, because it could be that the person you're interested in is interested in you as well, but is too shy or lacking in confidence to do anything about it. It's an awkward situation to be sure, and there's no guarantee you won't experience rejection, but that happens to everybody somewhere along the way. If you—both boys and girls—are interested in someone and want to move the relationship forward, go ahead and invite him or her to do something. It's often easier to simply include the person in a group activity with some of your friends rather than starting out one-on-one. You can keep it casual by saying something like, "a few of my friends and I are thinking of seeing *The Dark Knight* at the Imax theater Friday night. If you want to come along, we could pick you up on the way." The worst that he or she can say is "No," and chances are that you'll end up seeing a movie and having a good time together.

assume, however, that teens who are out on dates every weekend are experiencing happy, satisfying relationships.

Dating for the sake of dating can quickly become stressful, disappointing, and frustrating, and often results in feelings of emptiness or loneliness. Being with someone with whom you have little in common, or who wants to be with you only because you're considered by peers to be a desirable person to date, doesn't translate into a happy, healthy relationship, but often in an empty or superficial one.

Teens who rely on friends for social interaction rather than seeking short-term relationships just for the sake of having them are likely to experience less stress and more enjoyment than those who feel a need to be part of a superficial dating scene. When you do meet someone you like very much, and who likes you very much in return, you will bring with you a history of healthy, friendship-based relationships instead of the baggage of numerous, meaningless dating experiences.

It's important to remember that healthy relationships are based on far more than physical attraction, but include mutual respect and interest at many other levels.

Participating in a variety of activities that interest you will increase your chances of meeting and getting to know someone who shares your interests, and contributes to others having a more positive view of you. If you enjoy photography, for instance, and join the yearbook staff or enroll in a photo course, it's a pretty sure bet that you'll meet others who share your interest. Having a shared interest makes it easy to find something to talk about, and provides opportunities for spending time together.

Participating in something that interests you also helps to define who you are. Instead of just being "Tom," you're "Tom, the guy who takes the really cool pictures for the yearbook." Or, instead of being "Lindsey," you're "Lindsey, the girl who played the lead role in the school production of *Hairspray.*"

AVOIDING RISKY RELATIONSHIPS

Some teens, however, regardless of weight, report they're willing to go out with pretty much whoever asks them, even if they don't particularly like the person. They might go because they're afraid no one else will ask them, or they feel that dating anyone will improve their social status. You should be aware that there are people who look to befriend teens who are insecure, or lonely, or afraid that no one will like them, and then take advantage of them, sexually or otherwise.

Most everyone has a sort of radar system that lets us know when something is not right. You might feel uncomfortable or uneasy around someone without knowing why. You might feel that a date is coming on too strong, or pressuring you to do something you don't want to. If this happens to you, it's important to remember that it's not your fault, and that you have the right to say "no" and remove yourself from the situation.

Dating pressure is often directed toward sex, but can occur in other ways as well. Maybe someone is pressuring you to give him money, or to buy or keep illegal drugs or guns, or engage in other risky or illegal behavior. It helps to have a plan in place, just in case you ever find yourself in such a situation. Thinking about what you would say before such a situation ever arises can make you feel more prepared and confident in the event that it occurred. It's important to say no clearly and firmly so that you're not sending any mixed messages. If someone is pressuring you for sex, for instance, you simply need to say something like, "No. I'm not ready to have sex."

Sometimes a teen who doesn't want to have sex will try to avoid hurting a date's feelings by saying something like, "Well, I really want to, but I'm afraid I might catch something [meaning a sexually transmitted disease] if I do." This sends mixed messages and presents the opportunity for the person who's pressuring to continue doing so.

Another good idea is to have a plan in case you need to get out of a dating situation quickly. If you don't feel safe, you need to call someone you trust to help you by coming to get you. If you're in a situation that you feel is immediately dangerous, call 911 for help.

This information isn't intended to scare you or discourage you from seeking healthy relationships. The reality, however, is that you need to be aware and ready to take action if necessary. Study results that appeared in a 2001 edition of the *Journal of the American Medical Association* revealed that about one in five high school females reported having been physically or sexually abused by a dating partner.

RETHINKING BODY IMAGE

Most teens, including those who are not overweight, struggle with body image. Studies have shown that both boys and girls perceive themselves to be heavier than they really are. And weight is only one factor that contributes to body image.

You've demonstrated quite a bit of initiative by picking up this book and reading it. Hopefully, you've already started, or are getting ready to make some lifestyle changes that will result in improved health. You'll start feeling like you have more energy, which will allow you to be more physically active, which will result in better moods and self-esteem.

Still, chances are that you'll look in the mirror and sometimes wish you were seeing a body that's different from yours.

Just as our environment makes it challenging to maintain a healthy weight by offering a vast variety of easy-to-get, high-calorie foods, recreation space that often is limited or nonexistent, and sedentary entertainment in many different forms, unrealistic media images make it very difficult to achieve and maintain a healthy body image.

As the average weight of Americans is increasing, many of the people who are held up for our admiration on TV shows, in fashion shows, and in movies are getting thinner. Shows like *America's Next Top Model* and *Project Runway*, along with fashion magazines and catalogs, have brought super-thin models and perfect-body muscular men into our living rooms. It's the rare girl or woman who can watch the televised Victoria's Secret Fashion Show, during which beautiful, sexy models parade around in the least amount of lingerie permitted by the Federal Communications Commission, and feel good about how she looks.

Boys also are challenged on the issue of body image, bombarded with images of hip, muscular guys on music videos, sports programs, and celebrity shows. The message is put out for you very early on that you're supposed to look like they do, and when you don't, your body image suffers.

The fact is, however, that many people are beginning to question this media practice of portraying thin, perfect-body people as the norm, and with good reason. Nicole Richie, Michael Phelps, Usain Bolt, Kate Bosworth, and Paris Hilton defy the definition of normal as it applies to physical appearance.

People ranging from the editor in chief of *Glamour* magazine to fashion show organizers to health care providers are saying enough with the overly thin images that have become commonplace. Some fashion show and contest organizers have set minimum weight requirements to combat the unhealthy extremes that models and contestants pursue. *Glamour* editor in chief Cindi Leive said the magazine has an obligation to represent women of all sizes, and will not limit its models to size 2s and below.

When you get right down to it, there are no "perfect bodies." Different societies have different ideals, and ideals change over time. Try not to compare yourself with others, but to give yourself credit for the qualities you possess that you and others value, and continue working to improve your health and quality of life. And, remember, just as you don't like when others judge you by your appearance, don't judge yourself by your appearance either. You wouldn't accept that from others; don't accept it from yourself.

WHAT YOU NEED TO KNOW

➤ Tuning in to your health by monitoring how you feel and being aware of any changes that may occur is extremely important in the prevention and early detection of any sort of medical condition.

➤ Obesity can make personal care difficult, but there are strategies and products that can help you achieve and maintain good personal care.

➤ Once a problem for fashion-conscious teens, there are more and more shopping opportunities aimed at overweight and obese teenagers.

➤ You may feel left out of dating and relationships, but remember that the quality of a relationship is more meaningful than the number of dates or relationships, and that there are many kinds of meaningful relationships, not only those involving a couple.

➤ Understanding that hardly anybody meets the media standard of body size and appearance will help you to put less emphasis on your weight and shift your focus to other physical and personal qualities.

10

Helping Others Cope with Obesity

If you are overweight or obese, you no doubt have experienced some of the problems and issues associated with these conditions. It could be that you've been mocked and teased, or perhaps even physically provoked because of your condition. Maybe you feel really bad when you have to take a break because you're too winded to make it up a full flight of stairs, or you dread having to change in the locker room before gym class, or you feel like everyone is watching you in the cafeteria to see what you're eating. You might get really angry with a parent who suggests that you shouldn't have seconds while you're brother is already on his third helping of mashed potatoes, or upset with a friend who gives you a copy of a diet she found in a magazine.

If you've experienced these sorts of feelings, or other feelings that are related to being obese or overweight, you can be sure that other obese and overweight teens and adolescents have as well. As an obese or overweight teen, especially one who has taken the time to read this book, addressed the health issues discussed, and considered making behavioral changes for health improvement, you are in a unique position to help others who are struggling with the same kinds of problems.

EDUCATING OTHERS CONCERNING OBESITY

Sharing what you've learned from this book can be a great way to help others who are overweight or obese, and even those who aren't.

117

Obesity is a problem that we hear and read a lot about these days, but it was only in 2001 that the Surgeon General first called national attention to the obesity epidemic as a public health issue. While there is call now for institutional and societal efforts to combat the problem of obesity, many people still know very little about the reasons for obesity and how they can be addressed.

Among many non-obese people, there still are misconceptions and stereotypes regarding obesity that result in bias against those who are obese. Many still perceive that obese people are lazy or lacking in willpower or simply unwilling to address their weight issues. Having read this book, you know that obesity is a much more complicated problem, with no simple causes or solutions, and you have the power to help others understand that.

ABOUT OBESOGENIC ENVIRONMENTS

Way back in chapter 3 you read that many of us live in obesogenic environments—environments that generate or encourage obesity. In the same chapter, you read some suggestions for fighting back against those environments by working to make changes in your home, your school, and your community.

You could provide a service for others who are obese or overweight by sharing your knowledge about obesogenic environments and the steps that can be taken to change them. Some communities are beginning to look at how they can make where they live more accessible to walking and biking instead of using cars, or how they can assure better availability of fresh produce and other healthy foods as they limit the prevalence of fast-food restaurants. Many people, though, are still unaware of how where they live affects their health—and their weight.

Once you help others to understand how their environments work against them, you can ask them to join you in working to make positive changes, as suggested in chapter 3.

ABOUT PHYSICAL ACTIVITY

Physical activity is another topic about which you can work to educate others—particularly younger kids who may not have a positive role model in that area. We know that kids who are obese at preschool age have a 25 percent chance of becoming obese adults, that seven-year-olds who are obese have a 41 percent chance of obesity in adulthood, and obese 12-year-olds a 75 percent chance. It's vitally important for kids to get into good habits regarding physical activity (and other behaviors) early on to lessen the chance that they'll become obese in the first place. You can help by organizing fun activities that get them moving for the kids in your neighborhood, school, church, or community group. Recruit a couple of friends to help and, if you live in an area where it's possible, organize a bike ride or a hike. If not, plan a group trip to the playground or an indoor recreational area. Take a child out to the backyard and throw a ball or toss a Frisbee. You can serve as an excellent role model and mentor for a child who's already experiencing weight problems.

Take a few minutes to look over the behavioral theories discussed in chapter 6 and try to apply them when you're helping others. The learning theory, for instance, states that behaviors that result in positive consequences are more likely to be maintained than behaviors that result in negative consequences. If you know a child or another teen who is working toward making behavioral changes, you can use the learning theory by praising her when she makes a good choice, such as substituting a salad for french fries.

The social ecological model asserts that behavioral changes are dependent on our interactions with others and the choices you make are affected by the people with whom you spend time. By serving as a positive role model and making the right choices yourself, you can help someone else to make choices that may result in better health. It is very clear that children choose behaviors that they see others choose, especially those chosen by people they look up to, such as parents or older adolescents. That's why it's important to set a good example.

ABOUT NUTRITION AND ENERGY BALANCE

You've read a fair amount throughout this book about nutrition, which is another factor in the obesity equation about which you can help educate others. You've also read a lot about energy balance, an important concept in understanding why some people become obese and others don't.

Again, your efforts here may be directed particularly well toward younger kids, who may not know about food groups, the need for good nutrition, what foods provide the best nutrition, the calorie density of foods, and so forth. Some online resources you could share include the following:

▶ MyPyramid for Kids: www.mypyramid.gov/kids. Designed for kids six through 11, this site from the U.S. Department of Agriculture is intended to motivate them to make healthy choices concerning nutrition and physical activity. It includes tips for parents, coloring sheets, and a worksheet on which kids can keep track of their food choices and physical activities.

> BAM! Body and Mind: www.bam.gov. This site comes from the Centers for Disease Control and Prevention and is designed for nine- to 13-year-olds. It includes quizzes, games, and other interactive features to motivate kids, and has teacher's guides, as well.

> Eat Smart. Play Hard: www.fns.usda.gov/eatsmartplayhard. Also brought to you by the Department of Agriculture, this site features Power Panther and his nephew Slurp, who bring messages about nutrition and physical activity to young children.

> Small Step: www.smallstep.gov. This site includes games and activities, TV commercials urging kids to be active, a quiz, and other features. It's from the U.S. Department of Health and Human Services, and geared toward kids and adolescents.

> We Can!: wecan.nhlbi.nih.gov. Developed by the National Heart, Lung, and Blood Institute, We Can! (Ways to Enhance Children's Activity and Nutrition) is designed for families and communities to help kids maintain healthy weight. It stresses three major behaviors: improved food choices, increased physical activity, and decreased screen time.

EDUCATING OTHERS TO REDUCE BIAS AGAINST THE OBESE

Studies have revealed that obese people face bias and possible discrimination in at least three important areas of life: health care, education, and employment. Teachers, employers, medical workers, and even parents have been found to treat obese people—even their own kids—differently than those who aren't obese.

A first step toward combating these biases is to make people aware that they exist and that they may perpetuate them. Ask your family members or a friend to take the Implicit Association Test, which is described on page 46. This will help them to understand their own biases against obese people. Make sure to point out situations in which someone is exhibiting bias against an obese person, even if the person is doing so unconsciously.

Sharing information to help non-obese people better understand the complicated causes of obesity and why it's difficult for so many to

When dealing with someone who is obese, it's important to be aware of language that could be offensive or hurtful. "Excess weight" is a better term than "fatness" or "morbid obesity." The word "exercise" can be a turnoff, making "physical activity" a better choice. "Heaviness," "large size," "weight problem," and "excess fat" are words and phrases that give many obese people pause. Framing a discussion around the issue of promoting health, rather than treating obesity, sends a more positive message to a person who is trying to lose weight.

lose weight and keep it off may help them to be more understanding of issues associated with obesity, and help them to understand that obesity is more complicated than simply having too much food, too much sedentary activity, and too little physical activity.

This may not be an easy task, depending on whom you talk to, as some people can be very close-minded and mean-spirited regarding obesity and many other conditions. Other people, however, may welcome reliable information presented in a matter-of-fact manner. And remember, individuals exhibit bias and discrimination toward many groups of people who are different from them. It might help to know that other groups experience the same sorts of problems.

Areas that have received a fair amount of attention are language use as it relates to obesity, and the use of images that depict overweight and obese people in a negative manner, such as lying around or eating junk food. As we continue to learn and understand more about the causes and implications of obesity, we can hope that bias and discrimination against obese people will lessen.

PROVIDING SOCIAL SUPPORT

As an obese teenager, you get it. You understand what it's like to have somebody say something rude as you walk by, or to not be able to find fashionable clothing that fits you. Knowing what these things feel like enables you to be empathetic and offer support to others experiencing the same things. You can't, of course, totally understand other people's thoughts and feelings, but when you talk to them you can project understanding and *empathy*. Empathy, according to *Merriam-Webster's Collegiate Dictionary*, is "the action of understanding, being aware of, being sensitive to, and vicariously experiencing the feelings, thoughts, and experience of another of either the past or present without having the feelings, thoughts, and experience fully communicated in an objectively explicit manner."

That's a pretty long-winded way of saying that someone who is empathetic can understand what someone else is experiencing and feeling without the other person spelling it out for him, often because the empathetic person has been through a similar or identical situation.

Human beings are social animals, and we all need and desire some degree of social support. Social support is both physical and emotional, and it comes from our families, friends, peers, coworkers, teachers, and others. It can be as small as a pat on the back, or as big as a sharing of innermost feelings. It helps us to feel that we are accepted as part of a group and to deal with stressful situations.

If you know someone who is struggling for any reason, but particularly because of issues associated with obesity, you can help by offering social support. There are several forms of social support, including emotional support, informational support, sharing feelings, giving and receiving personal feedback, and giving and receiving practical help.

Take a few minutes to consider how you might offer these types of social support to a friend or family member, or even to someone you don't know very well but suspect may benefit from some support. Emotional support can be presented in the form of a hug, a touch on the arm, an offer to talk, or sometimes just a smile. Letting someone know that you understand she's struggling is a form of support, as is sharing your feelings and letting her know you're open to hearing how she's feeling. Sharing your experiences and how you coped with problems are good means of social support, as is providing actual help when necessary.

RECOGNIZING WHEN SOMEONE NEEDS HELP

We all travel through rough stretches of life, and we all need a hand up from time to time. Teenage years can be particularly stressful due to pressures to fit in, to achieve, to figure out where your life is heading, and so on. Sometimes, though, serious problems occur that need to be recognized and dealt with, because significant consequences can result if they're not. The sections below explain how to best deal with and help someone who is facing a difficult situation, such as bullying or depression.

Bullying. We know that 30 percent of girls and 25 percent of boys reported being bullied in a survey of obese teens conducted in Minneapolis, making bullying a very real problem among this population. You read tips from experts at the Yale University Rudd Center for Food Policy and Obesity for dealing with bullying in chapter 5, but it's also important to know how to help a friend who's being bullied.

First, remember that there are various forms of bullying: physical, teasing, and intentional exclusion. While physical bullying requires the most immediate action, all forms of it can be hurtful and destructive.

If you have a friend or maybe a younger brother or sister who's being bullied, there are steps you can take to help.

> ➤ Be supportive and find out all you can regarding the situation. When is the bullying occurring? How many people are involved? Is there a physical threat?
> ➤ Don't blame your friend or sibling.
> ➤ Be empathetic. Share any experiences you might have had, and assure your friend or sibling that something can be done.

Shawn Andrews, a six-feet-four-inch, 335-pound football guard with the Philadelphia Eagles, recently revealed that he'd been diagnosed with clinical depression, and that he believes he can trace his problems back to extensive teasing about his weight when he was a child. In a recent interview with a Philadelphia TV station, Andrews, 26, recalled that kids made fun of him because of his size starting in first grade, and that in third grade the entire playground jumped him. Members of the mental health community applauded Andrews's willingness to talk about his illness and his decision to seek treatment. Depression is generally believed to be caused by brain chemistry, family history, and emotional environment, meaning that Andrews was "wired" in a way that contributed to his condition. His recollection of the teasing, however, revealed how hurtful it had been and how it can have very serious long-term consequences, and shows us that even successful celebrities have experienced emotional problems associated with overweight and obesity.

> Don't encourage retaliation, either physically or with words. This only causes the situation to escalate.
> Don't become overly emotional about what's happening with your sibling or friend. You're in a better position to help if you can remain calm.
> Stick with your friend or sibling and try to get others to join you. There's safety in numbers and chances are the bully will soon lose interest.
> Talk to a teacher, the principal, your friend's parent, or another trusted adult. You may have to do this sometimes even if your friend doesn't want you to. It's better to have your friend be angry with you than to be seriously hurt or intimidated by a bully.

Depression. Depression can affect anyone, but obesity increases the risk of developing depression, according to the U.S. Department of Health and Human Services. If you suspect that someone you care about is suffering from depression (see page 52 for a list of common symptoms), it's important that you try to get her to talk about it, and more importantly, to see a doctor or counselor. Depression is a treatable condition, but it has to be acknowledged in order to be treated.

You can support a depressed friend by offering to go with her to talk to the school counselor or nurse or another trusted adult. You can continue to be her friend by asking her to do things that you've enjoyed in the past, and by being patient, understanding, and encouraging. Someone who is depressed might feel empty and tired, and have a hard time imagining that her situation will ever improve. Be positive (but not overly cheery) and talk about things you'll do in the future. Assure her that you're her friend, and let her know you're there for her.

While you can support your friend, you can't substitute for a doctor or counselor, and you should never keep a serious issue like depression a secret, not even if your friend asks you to. If you're worried about your friend, you need to find an adult you trust and share your concerns.

Suicide. If you suspect a friend is considering suicide, you need to act immediately. One of the major risks of depression is suicide, which is the third leading cause of death among those between 15 and 24 years old. Take a minute to refresh yourself on the symptoms of suicide risk found in the sidebar on page 54. If you feel your friend is experiencing some of all of those symptoms, you need to tell an adult immediately. Encourage her to call the National Suicide Prevention Lifeline, a toll-free, 24-hour hotline that is staffed by trained counselors. The number is (800) 273-TALK. If your friend is in immediate danger of harming herself, call 911.

Substance abuse and other risky behaviors. Risky behaviors, including use of drugs and alcohol, driving after using drugs or alcohol, engaging in unsafe sex, possessing a weapon or engaging in violent activities, and not using a seatbelt can also result from depression. If someone you know is exhibiting risky behavior, you should first address the issue with him, and then, if the behavior doesn't change, with an adult.

This can be a very difficult task, because no one wants to tell on a friend or get someone into trouble. If risky behavior is putting your friend at risk, however, the best thing you can do as a friend is to let a responsible adult know about it.

WHAT YOU NEED TO KNOW

> ‣ You can help others who are obese by helping them to know more about the problems and factors associated with obesity.
> ‣ Teaching others about how their environments affect their weight, the importance of physical activity, and how what they eat contributes to energy balance or imbalance can help them to think about their weight and perhaps begin to make positive behavioral changes.
> ‣ Teaching children about nutrition and exercise is extremely important, particularly for those who don't have good role models in those areas.
> ‣ Education also is important for non-obese people, many of whom harbor misconceptions and even bad feelings against those who are obese.
> ‣ Providing social support to obese friends and family members is another critical way that you can help.
> ‣ It's really important to know when a friend or family member has a problem that you and she can't solve on your own, and be willing to step up to get adult help at that point.

11

Paying for Care

While the condition of obesity is a problem, the issue of paying for treatment for obesity can also be worrisome. The rising obesity rate in the United States has many policy makers worried as its consequences threaten to overburden the country's health care system, the resources of which already are stretched thin.

It's ironic that many insurers will not cover obesity treatment, or programs that may help to prevent obesity, but most cover treatment necessary for obesity-related illnesses and disorders, such as diabetes or sleep apnea.

More than 45 million Americans are uninsured, and many people with employer-provided health plans are being asked to pay more in deductibles and other costs. This means an increasing number of Americans are relying on publicly funded care, or simply not getting the care that they should. While health care plans for children are available, meaning that no child should be left without health insurance, the plans may be difficult to access because of complicated application processes. Health experts and policy makers are working to figure out how to solve these problems as they anticipate an increasing number of obesity-related health problems in the future.

You read in earlier chapters of this book that the primary treatments for obesity are decreasing energy consumption and increasing energy output. While it's possible to achieve those things on your own at little or no cost, many people find that they're more successful when they participate in a weight loss program or seek advice from a health professional.

In fact, many medical experts now recommend a combination of professional medical care and community-based efforts—such as improved school lunches and community physical activity centers—for the treatment of obesity, with the ultimate goal of family or self-management of the condition.

Insurance companies and plans, however, vary in their willingness to pay for components of obesity treatment, which could include some or all of the steps listed below:

> ➤ Assessment of diet and physical activity levels
> ➤ Screening for current medical conditions and future risks
> ➤ Nutritional counseling
> ➤ Gym membership or other physical activity programs
> ➤ Participation in a behavior modification–based weight management program
> ➤ Medications
> ➤ Weight control surgery

Normally, insurers will cover a visit to a primary care provider for someone seeking obesity treatment. If the primary provider feels that obesity is an issue, he or she may refer you to a nutritionist for nutritional counseling, and, perhaps recommend that you seek the services of a physical therapist or occupational therapist to help you with issues regarding activity. Your primary care provider might also refer you to a psychologist or social worker to help you change your habits. Sometimes, insurers will pay for some or all of those follow-up services.

A study of 16 insurance providers in Pennsylvania revealed limited coverage for tools promoting lifestyle modification, such as physical activity programs or physician-monitored diets. About half the providers paid for nutritional counseling, but only one reimbursed for weight loss drugs. All of the providers, however, were willing to at least partially pay for weight loss surgery, a willingness that is not shared by all insurance companies, especially when teens are involved. Experts are hopeful that insurers will become more willing to reimburse for obesity treatment before weight loss surgery is needed, as the companies become increasingly aware of the health benefits of losing even just a little bit of weight, and see that lifestyle modification is an important tool in weight loss.

The Centers for Medicare and Medicaid Services, which runs programs that provide health insurance for the elderly, people with disabilities, and some low-income people, changed its policy in 2004 of not usually covering weight loss programs and therapies. That didn't mean that all weight loss therapies would automatically be covered, but it did allow for patients and health care providers to at least apply for coverage. It varies from state to state, but in some states Medicaid and Medicare provide coverage for obesity treatment and prevention, especially for children and adolescents. However, in areas where Medicaid is administered by managed-care companies, the benefits will vary.

Advocates for insurance coverage of obesity treatment were heartened by the Medicare decision to cover surgery and some changes in state Medicaid benefits, since private insurance companies often follow the lead of those agencies.

UNDERSTANDING HEALTH INSURANCE OPTIONS

Health insurance isn't something that teens typically spend much time thinking about. If you desire medical treatment for obesity and your family can't afford to pay for it, however, it may become an important issue to you. Let's take a brief look at the major programs and types of insurance available.

Employment-based health insurance. This is when health insurance is provided as a job benefit to employees and their families. *Employment-based health insurance* may be provided at no cost to employees, although most companies require workers to share some of the costs in the form of premium payments, co-pays, or deductibles. Coverage may vary tremendously under this broad umbrella of insurance, depending on the type of policy. A *health maintenance organization,* or HMO, for instance, generally requires approval for many services that would automatically be covered with another type of plan, such as a *preferred provider organization* (PPO) or a *point of service* (POS) plan. HMOs only cover care provided by approved health care providers who participate in the HMO's plan and adhere to its guidelines and restrictions. PPOs are more flexible and usually allow you to choose which health care providers you wish to use, while POSs are sort of combinations of HMOs and PPOs. POSs allow you to see any provider you want, but you'll pay more out of pocket if the provider isn't part of the network.

Privately purchased health insurance. Someone who does not work, works for a company that doesn't provide health insurance, or is self-employed may need to purchase his own insurance. What insurance is available and for how much varies from state to state. Insurance costs much more in some states than in others.

Government-funded health care coverage. People who don't have jobs that provide health insurance and can't afford to buy their own may qualify for Medicaid or the *State Children's Health Insurance Program* (SCHIP), which covers anyone who qualifies up to age 18. In 2007, 83 million people were covered by *government-funded health care,* including 23 million children. Still, more than 8 million children remained without health insurance, according to government statistics.

If your family is a low-income family and doesn't have any health insurance, you might qualify for government-funded health care coverage. Medicaid is a federal program, but it's administered by each state, which means that requirements for eligibility vary from state to state. Also, depending on where you live, you may receive Medicaid coverage through a managed-care organization. You can learn more about who is eligible for Medicaid at www.cms.hhs.gov/medicaid/eligibility or http://www.cms.hhs.gov/whoiseligible.asp. More information about the SCHIP program is available at www.cms.hhs.gov/schip or www.insurekidsnow.gov. You can also learn more by calling (877) KIDS-NOW.

If you are 18 or younger and do not have health insurance, you should know that you often have the right to coverage. Children can be covered by Medicaid in some states; in families where parents don't qualify for Medicaid but can't afford to buy health insurance, children should be covered by SCHIP.

MEDICAL CARE FACILITIES

Medical care is provided in different types of facilities, including medical offices, health clinics, community health centers, and hospitals. Doctors in private practice normally expect payment from patients at the time that services are provided, or will bill their patients' insurers for payment. If the services doctors provide are not covered by insurance, doctors may be understandably reluctant to perform them.

That doesn't mean that doctors don't provide necessary treatment for patients without guarantee of insurance reimbursement—they do so all the time. If a service is not necessary and not covered, however, a doctor may decline to provide it, or ask the patient to pay up front or sign a promise to pay any bills that result from the service.

Figuring out whether or not your private insurance will pay for a particular service can be a daunting task. Some plans, for instance, will cover consultation with a nutritionist, while other plans don't. Even if your insurance will cover the consultation, however, it may only do so if you go to a nutritionist who participates in the plan. It's a good idea to find out in advance if a service will be covered by checking your plan's benefit agreement and directories of service providers. Medical care is expensive, and many families have gotten into financial difficulty due to medical bills. If you're not sure if a service is covered, ask a parent to check into the matter by reviewing the policy or calling the insurance company.

If your family can't afford to go to a doctor in a private practice because of insurance or financial concerns, you can obtain medical care at a health clinic or community health center. Most cities have clinics or community health centers, as do an increasing number of small towns and rural areas.

Some clinics are run by hospitals, while others are sponsored by cities and funded largely by the federal government. Often patients who don't have insurance are billed on a sliding scale, depending on their income and the size of their families. No one who needs medical care is turned away, even if he has no income or insurance.

Community health centers, funded by the Health Resources and Services Administration (HRSA), are another option for free or reduced-cost health care. These centers vary greatly in their scope and services, but are typically well-run and quite successful. Organized by community-based, usually not-for-profit, health organizations and funded by grants from HRSA, which is a division of the U.S. Department of Health and Human Services, there are thousands of these centers throughout the country, both in urban and rural areas that are considered medically underserved. These are areas in which the number of private doctors and health care providers is insufficient to care for the needs of the local population, which are not necessarily low-income areas. Typically, people who work at these community health centers are very dedicated to the health of the local population and do a great job at providing high-quality care, in particular preventive care, even if the health center itself is not luxurious. Because the centers are not under pressure to turn over large profits, they often offer better preventive care than even private practice, and are generally well regarded.

A prime example of a community health care organization is the Community Health Care Association of New York State (CHCANYS), an organization founded in 1971 by community members looking to care for underserved populations. CHCANYS oversees 50 community health centers, with 425 sites throughout New York City and around the state.

A well-regarded example of a community health center is the Kansas City Free Health Clinic, founded in 1971. With two locations serving Kansas City, the free clinic served more than 45,000 patients during its 2006–07 fiscal year and provided nearly 27,000 free prescription medications. The clinic has a professional staff of 64 full-time employees along with more than 600 volunteers. It is funded by multiple sources, including HRSA and other grants, private donations, the United Way, and special events, and is housed in two modern, attractive, well-equipped buildings in different parts of the city.

If you need to find low-cost or no-cost health care, you or your parents can check with HRSA, which maintains a nationwide directory of clinics. More information about HRSA is available on its Web site at www.ask.hrsa.gov. By typing in your state, city, and zip code and the type of facility in which you're interested, you'll be given a list of clinics in your area. Or go to your city's Web site or search for clinics in the city or neighborhood in which you live. Just remember that obesity treatment is often not available, regardless of what type of health care facility you approach.

HRSA also provides a list of Hill-Burton obligated hospitals and other health care facilities that, because they have received government grants and loans for construction and modernization, are required to provide a certain amount of free and low cost health care. You can find these facilities on the HRSA Web site, or call the Hill-Burton hotline at (800) 638-0742.

Another option may be participation in an academic institution–based research study, which typically does not cost anything. You'll sometimes see ads for these studies in a local newspaper, or you can look for active trials at www.clinicaltrials.gov.

Or, look for community-based weight loss programs sponsored by organizations such as YMCAs or recreational facilities. These often are offered for free or at affordable rates. Be aware, however, that the quality of such programs varies greatly, so try to find out in advance what the program entails and make sure it will be worth your investment.

MEDICATION COSTS

If a doctor prescribes you one of the two weight loss medications that have been approved for adolescents and teens and you can't afford to buy the medicine, you have several options. You or your parents can ask your doctor for free medication samples. Most doctors are happy to provide samples if they have them. A longer-term solution, though, is to apply for free medications from the pharmaceutical companies that manufacture them. Most drug companies offer these to patients who can't afford them through a variety of assistance programs. Your parents may have to fill out some paperwork and provide proof of financial need in order to qualify, and your doctor will usually be required to write a note for you.

You can find out more about free drug programs on the Web sites of the pharmaceutical companies that make the drugs you need. If your doctor prescribed Meridia, for instance, you should go the Web site of Abbot Laboratories, which manufactures that drug. Allī, another kind of approved weight loss drug, is manufactured by GlaxoSmithKline.

Some Web sites where you can learn more about obtaining reduced rate or free prescription drugs are listed below.

> ▸ Partnership for Prescription Assistance: www.pparx.org
> ▸ Prescription Drug Assistance Programs: www.phrma.org
> ▸ R_x Outreach: www.rxassist.org

WHAT YOU NEED TO KNOW

> ▸ Paying for health care is a problem for many, many Americans struggling with increasing costs and, in some cases, declining insurance coverage.

Remember that while weight loss medications can be helpful, they don't work unless they're used properly and in conjunction with behavioral treatment. You can't rely on drugs alone to achieve weight loss, so that shouldn't be your priority in looking for obesity treatment.

➤ Even if your family has a good insurance plan, many treatments and services applicable to obesity are not covered.
➤ Health insurance can be provided by an employer, purchased privately, or provided by the government.
➤ If you can't afford medical treatment from a physician in a private practice, check to see if there are any free or reduced-fee health clinics or community health centers available in your area.
➤ You may be eligible for free medications if they are prescribed to you and you can't afford them.

APPENDIX

Online Resources

Action for Healthy Kids
www.actionforhealthykids.org
Founded in 2002, Action for Healthy Kids is a nonprofit organization made up of more than 60 national organizations and government agencies that work in the areas of health, fitness, and nutrition. Although it is a nonprofit organization, some of its largest contributors are for-profit companies (Kraft Foods, Kellogg's), or are organizations (the National Dairy Council, the Entertainment Industry Foundation) with a vested interest in shaping the perception of the childhood obesity problem. The organization focuses on improving nutritional standards and physical activity levels in schools.

Active Living by Design
www.activelivingbydesign.org
Active Living by Design is a national program, funded by the Robert Wood Johnson Foundation, a large philanthropic organization devoted to health and health care. Active Living by Design proposes and implements innovative ways to increase physical activity and healthy food availability through community design. It also addresses public policy regarding health and works to make people more aware of issues concerning health and health care. The site includes information about events and publications, active living programs, and case studies about healthy eating.

America on the Move
www.americaonthemove.org
With a message of making small changes for improved health, America on the Move provides interactive tools, challenges to increase the number of steps taken each day and decrease the number of calories consumed, a tip of the day, and personalized online resources. Although a nonprofit organization, some of its largest contributors

are for-profit companies (PepsiCo, Nestlé) with a vested interest in shaping the perception of the childhood obesity problem.

America Walks
www.americawalks.org

America Walks is a national organization dedicated to making communities across the country more friendly to walking. Its mission is to empower people on the local level to become advocates for walkable communities, to educate the public on the importance of such communities, and to provide a voice for advocates of walking. The site offers resources for anyone interested in starting an advocacy group in his community, and has a speaker's bureau.

BAM! Body and Mind
www.bam.gov

Created by the Centers for Disease Control and Prevention, BAM! is designed for kids ages nine to 13. It includes quizzes, games, and other interactive features to motivate kids, and has teacher's guides and information for parents as well.

CalorieKing
www.calorieking.com

CalorieKing offers users calorie and nutritional information for thousands of different foods. It also contains other useful features.

ClinicalTrials.gov
www.clinicaltrials.gov

ClinicalTrials.gov is a listing of clinical trials being conducted in the United States and in other countries. The trials are both publicly and privately supported. The site includes information about the purpose of each trial, who may be eligible to participate, trial locations, and contact information. The site is a service of the U.S. National Institutes of Health.

The Community Tool Box
www.ctb.ku.edu

The Community Tool Box was designed and is operated by the Work Group for Community Health and Development at the University of Kansas. It's the world's largest free resource for people who want to acquire the necessary skills to contribute to the building of healthy communities. The Community Tool Box is recognized *as a global resource for those looking to improve the places where they live.*

Cookbook of Healthy Recipes
www.chop.edu/healthycookbook
The Children's Hospital of Philadelphia's Healthy Weight Program has released the second edition of Nutrition in the Kitchen, *a downloadable cookbook with recipes for appetizers, main dishes, side dishes, snacks and beverages, and desserts.*

Eat Smart. Play Hard.
www.fns.usda.gov/eatsmartplayhard
Eat Smart. Play Hard is a U.S. Department of Agriculture Web site for kids, featuring Power Panther and his nephew Slurp, who deliver messages about nutrition and physical activity in hopes of making kids more aware of behaviors at an early age.

Healthy Places
www.cdc.gov/healthyplaces
Healthy Places is a Centers for Disease Control and Prevention site that focuses on issues such as community design, poorly planned growth, healthy environments, and what can be done to create healthy places and discourage non-healthy ones. It addresses issues such as accessibility, children's health and the built environment, physical activity, and respiratory health and air pollution. The site, which was launched in 2001, includes a health impact assessment tool that allows you to get an idea of how your community stacks up, and links to other sources addressing these and similar topics.

Healthy Weight—It's Not a Diet, It's a Lifestyle
www.cdc.gov/nccdphp/dnpa/healthyweight/index.htm
Healthy Weight is a resource of the Centers for Disease Control and Prevention that provides a body mass index calculator, healthy tips for parents, and a lot of information about calories, physical activities, medical conditions related to obesity, and much more.

Implicit Association Test
implicit.harvard.edu
This site contains tests that measure attitudes toward various groups of people, including those who are obese. It uses a high-speed word association exercise intended to give participants a better idea of their attitudes toward people who are obese or overweight. Many

people don't recognize that they're prejudiced against obese people. In fact, many obese people have the same weight bias against other obese people as the rest of the population. The test, which takes about 20 minutes to complete, can help you to discover whether you are biased against overweight or obese people.

International Size Acceptance Association
www.size-acceptance.org
The mission of the International Size Acceptance Association (ISAA) is to promote size acceptance and fight size discrimination throughout the world. ISAA's primary purpose is to end the most common form of size discrimination and bigotry against obese children and adults. ISAA defines size discrimination as any action that places people at a disadvantage simply because of their size. This association is perceived as controversial by some due its militant character.

Living XL
www.livingXL.com
Living XL is geared entirely toward making life more comfortable for plus-sized customers. You can shop for products ranging from patio furniture to car and airplane seat belt extenders. A sampling of products includes scales that accommodate up to 1,000 pounds, a heavy-duty camp cot, travel belts in sizes up to 72, durable hammocks, a full line of clothing, and much more.

MedlinePlus
www.medlineplus.gov
MedlinePlus is a consumer database compiled by the U.S. National Library of Medicine, a division of the National Institutes of Health. The site will direct you to information from reliable sources to help answer health questions, gives you access to articles from medical journals, and contains extensive information about drugs, an illustrated medical encyclopedia, interactive patient tutorials, and relevant health news.

Mindless Eating: Why We Eat More than We Think
www.mindlesseating.org
Mindless Eating explores the research of Brian Wansink, Ph.D., director of the Food and Brand Laboratory at Cornell University. It includes a mindless eating challenge, forums, a blog, and reports on some of Wansink's innovative studies and research projects.

MyPyramid

www.mypyramid.gov

MyPyramid is a comprehensive site from the U.S. Department of Agriculture that provides personalized eating plans for users, interactive features such as a menu planner and an energy balance analyzer, information about the nutritional values of various foods, and many other useful components.

MyPyramid for Kids

www.mypyramid.gov/kids

Designed for kids ages six through 11, this site is a simplified version of the MyPyramid site described above. MyPyramid for Kids is intended to motivate them to make healthy choices concerning nutrition and physical activity. It includes tips for parents, coloring sheets, and a worksheet on which kids can keep track of their food choices and physical activities.

National Association for Health and Fitness

www.physicalfitness.org

The National Association for Health and Fitness is a nonprofit group that champions physical fitness, sports, and healthy lifestyles. The site offers information about the network of state governor's councils on physical fitness and sports for every state and U.S. territory.

The Obesity Society

www.obesity.org

The Obesity Society is a nonprofit organization and the leading scientific society dedicated to the study of obesity. Its mission is, through research, education, and advocacy, to better understand, prevent, and treat obesity and improve the lives of those affected. It supports work to prevent obesity; advocates for appropriate insurance coverage for obesity treatment; and promotes policy to stop discrimination against obese people. It also supports professionals who care for obese people. The Obesity Society's fundraising component, the American Obesity Association Research Foundation, raises money to support obesity related academic research. The Obesity Society holds an annual scientific meeting, and publishes a peer-reviewed journal, Obesity. *The Obesity Society's Web site includes statistics and facts, educational materials, and access to the online version of the journal.*

Overeaters Anonymous

www.oa.org

Overeaters Anonymous offers a program of recovery from compulsive overeating using the Twelve Steps and Twelve Traditions. Worldwide meetings and other tools provide a fellowship of experience, strength, and hope where members respect one another's anonymity. OA charges no dues or fees; it is self-supporting through member contributions. Unlike other organizations that deal with overweight, OA is not just about weight loss, obesity, or diets; it addresses physical, emotional, and spiritual well-being. It is not a religious organization and does not promote any particular diet. To address weight loss, OA encourages members to develop a food plan with a health care professional and a sponsor.

School Health Index

apps.nccd.cdc.gov/shi/default.aspx

The School Health Index, created by the Centers for Disease Control and Prevention, allows you to assess your school in order to get an idea of its strengths and shortcomings regarding various components of health, including nutrition, health education, physical education, and physical activity programs. The index addresses physical activity, healthy eating, tobacco use, safety, and asthma, and is intended to involve school administration, faculty, students, and community members in planning and instituting healthy changes in their schools.

Small Step

www.smallstep.gov

This site includes games and activities, TV commercials urging kids to be active, a health tip of the day, daily quiz, an activity tracker, video contest, and other features. It's from the U.S. Department of Health and Human Services, and geared toward kids, adolescents, and adults.

Walking School Bus

www.walkingschoolbus.org

Walking School Bus contains all you need to know to get a walking bus up and running in your neighborhood. It includes checklists of what to do to get started, hazards to avoid, how to assure the safety of walkers, reports regarding walking buses in other areas, the benefits of having children walk or bike to school, and much more. It also includes information on the Bicycle Train, a variation of the Walking School Bus, where kids ride bikes to school as a group.

WebMD

www.webmd.com

WebMD is a highly regarded Web site that provides information on a wide variety of health-related issues, including diet and physical activity, mental health, medications, and medical conditions. It also offers tools to help you locate a doctor, create a custom plan for weight loss, and identify symptoms, as well as blogs and message boards.

We Can!

www.nhlbi.nih.gov/health/public/heart/obesity/wecan

We Can! is a Web site developed by the National Heart, Lung, and Blood Institute. We Can! (which stands for Ways to Enhance Children's Activity and Nutrition) is designed for families, health professionals, and communities to help kids maintain healthy weight. It stresses three major behaviors: improved food choices, increased physical activity, and decreased screen time. Users can access a variety of information, resources, and materials.

YMCA of the USA

ymca.net

The YMCA is the largest not-for-profit community service organization in the country, offering programs in fitness, health, child care, and much more. The YMCA of the USA site contains general information about the organization, along with a listing of YMCA locations to help you locate one near your home.

GLOSSARY

adolescent psychiatrist   A psychiatrist who is specially trained to work with young people.

assistive device   A tool designed to help with a particular task, such as reaching for an object on the floor, pulling on socks, or washing a hard-to-reach spot on your back.

asthma   A chronic disease that causes narrowing of the airways that carry oxygen to the lungs, often causing discomfort and requiring frequent treatment.

behavioral economics theory   A change theory that states behaviors are largely based on economic factors, and that people are more likely to choose healthier foods when the prices of less healthy foods are increased, or when less healthy foods are unavailable.

behavior change   Doing things differently than how you did them in the past.

Blount's disease   A disorder that causes a bowlegged appearance and, left untreated, can progress until it becomes difficult or impossible to walk.

body image   The perception that a person has concerning his or her body, which may or may not be accurate.

body mass index (BMI)   The most common standard used to determine overweight or obesity in teenagers.

brand placement   A form of advertising in which certain products appear within the content of a show instead of during a commercial.

built environment   All buildings, spaces and products that are created or modified by people. The built environment includes homes, schools, workplaces, parks, recreation areas, greenways, business areas, and transportation systems. [. . .] It includes land-use planning and policies that impact our communities in urban, rural, and suburban areas (definition provided by the National Institutes of Health).

calorie   A unit of measurement for energy.

141

cholesterol   A type of fat that can accumulate in the body and is linked to cardiovascular diseases.

comfort foods   Foods that make us feel good when we eat them, but often are calorie dense with little nutritional value.

common obesity   The great majority of obesity that is not caused by medical reasons.

Cushing's syndrome   A condition caused by prolonged exposure to high levels of cortisol, a hormone manufactured within the body by the adrenal glands, that can result in obesity.

depression   An illness characterized by hopelessness and negative perceptions of oneself and of the world. Depression involves the body, mood, and thoughts, and affects the way a person eats and sleeps, the way one feels about oneself, and the way one thinks about things.

diabetes   A disorder of metabolism, which is the way our bodies use digested food for growth and energy. Diabetes may be type 1, which is an autoimmune disease and not related to obesity; type 2, which is the most prevalent type among adults and is associated with obesity; and gestational diabetes, which occurs only in pregnant women.

diffusion theory   A theory that outlines how technological ideas expand from being created to being used within society.

eating disorder   An illness that can result in a pattern of harmful eating habits.

empathy   The ability to understand what someone else is feeling, thinking, or experiencing.

employment-based health insurance   Health insurance that is provided as a benefit to an employee and usually to his or her family.

empty calories   Calories contained in foods that offer little or no nutritional benefit.

energy   The calories contained in what we eat and drink.

energy balance   The process of consuming about as many calories as are used for a person to stay alive, grow, and participate in daily activities.

energy expenditure   The energy your body uses up for maintaining itself, growing, and moving.

energy imbalance   The process of consuming many more calories than you use, or using up many more calories than you consume.

energy intake   The energy you consume in the form of calories.

fatty liver disease   The condition of fat deposits in the liver, which can eventually cause inflammation, cirrhosis, and liver failure.

gallstones A condition that occurs when cholesterol and other materials contained in bile, a substance produced by the liver to help digest fats, harden to form stones.

gastric banding A form of weight loss surgery in which a silicone band is placed around the upper part of the stomach, creating a pouch that reduces the amount of food the stomach can hold.

gastric bypass surgery A common form of weight loss surgery, in which a small pouch is created at the top of the stomach and the rest of the stomach is sealed off.

gastroesophageal reflux A condition that occurs when stomach contents flow back into the esophagus, causing severe pain and discomfort and the possibility of damage to the esophagus or esophageal cancer.

gene The basic biological unit of heredity.

genetics The scientific study of heredity.

government-funded health care Health care supported by government programs for people who can't afford their own insurance and meet other requirements.

health maintenance organization (HMO) A type of insurance plan which covers care provided by approved health care providers who participate in the HMO's plan and agrees to its guidelines and restrictions.

high blood pressure Also known as hypertension, high blood pressure is a medical condition that causes the heart to work harder to pump blood to the body and contributes to cardiovascular disease, stroke, eye problems, and kidney disease.

high calorie density foods Foods that contain a lot of calories, even in small servings, such as butter, nuts, bacon, and french fries.

hypothyroidism A condition in which the thyroid doesn't produce enough hormones, upsetting the balance of chemical reactions within the body. In some instances, obesity can result. Also known as underactive thyroid disease.

insulin A hormone secreted by the pancreas, an organ located behind the stomach, which regulates the use of sugar in the body.

insulin resistance A condition in which cells in the body do not respond as well as normal to insulin, resulting in problem with the use of sugar in the body.

learning theory The theory that behaviors that result in positive consequences are more likely to be maintained than behaviors that result in negative consequences.

left ventricular hypertrophy An increased thickness of the heart's main pumping chamber, it increases the possibility of heart disease.

leptin A protein hormone produced by the fat tissue in the body that is necessary for regulating energy balance.

leptin deficiency A rare condition in which not enough leptin is produced within the body, resulting in a person being able to eat tremendous amounts of food and still feel hungry.

low calorie density foods Foods that contain few calories, even in large amounts, such as lettuce, vegetable soup, broiled fish, and oranges.

Medicaid A federal program that provides health care coverage to people who meet its qualifications. Medicaid is administered through each state government.

metabolic problems A group of conditions, including type 2 diabetes, insulin resistance, and metabolic syndrome.

metabolic syndrome A group of risk factors that increase chances of heart disease, problems with blood vessels, and diabetes.

metabolism The process the body uses to convert food to energy.

obesity An excess of body fat that is associated with health problems.

obesogenic environment An environment that generates obesity.

occupational therapist A therapist who works with patients to help them be more able to accomplish tasks of living, such as walking, washing, dressing, or cooking.

orlistat One of two weight loss medications approved for adolescents and teens, orlistat is in a class of drugs called lipase inhibitors. It works in the intestines by blocking the digestion of some fats.

osteoarthritis A condition that occurs when cartilage, a rubbery material that covers the end of bones in the joints, breaks down and loses its ability to cushion the joints. Osteoarthritis, also called degenerative joint disease, can occur in nearly any joint in the body, but is most common in the knees, hips, and spine.

pedometer A device that records the number of steps taken by detecting the motion of the hips.

point of service (POS) A type of health insurance that allows patients to choose any health care provider they want, but charges more out of pocket if the provider is not part of the plan's network.

polycystic ovary syndrome (PCOS) A condition linked to obesity and characterized by missed or irregular menstrual periods and increased levels of testosterone (a male hormone) in girls. It is the leading cause of infertility among women in the United States.

portion The amount of food that you would normally eat at one time.

preferred provider organization (PPO) A type of health insurance that generally is flexible in allowing patients to choose their own health care providers.

privately purchased health insurance   Health insurance obtained and paid for by an individual or family.

risky behaviors   Intentional actions that may result in harm or lead to harm.

sedentary activity   Any activity that does not require you to move, such as watching TV, chatting online, or playing video or computer games.

self-esteem   The attitude one has regarding himself or herself.

self-monitoring   Being aware of and keeping track of particular behaviors in an intentional manner.

serving   A standardized amount of food.

sibutramine   One of two weight loss medications that have been approved for adolescents and teens. Sibutramine is one of a class of medications called appetite suppressants, which means it acts on appetite control centers in the brain to make you feel less hungry.

sleep apnea   A medical condition characterized by irregular breathing, snoring, and poor quality of sleep.

slipped capital femoral epiphyses (SCFE)   A disorder of the hip where there is a separation of the ball of the hip joint and the upper end of the thigh bone, or femur.

social ecological model   A theory that states behavioral choices are dependent on our interactions with others over a period of time, and that the choices we make are affected by those with whom we interact.

social learning theory   A behavioral theory that asserts behaviors are influenced by the company you keep.

State Children's Health Insurance Program (SCHIP)   A publicly funded health insurance program for children up to 18 years of age who are not otherwise covered.

support person   An individual who works with you and assists in your weight loss efforts.

transtheoretical model of change   A model of behavior change that includes five stages leading up to, accomplishing, and maintaining change.

triglycerides   A type of fat that circulates or is stored in the body and is linked to insulin resistance and cardiovascular diseases.

weight-based discrimination   Unfair treatment based on a person's appearance and weight status.

weight cycling   The undesirable process of losing, gaining, losing, and gaining weight.

READ MORE ABOUT IT

American Academy of Pediatrics, and Sandra G. Hassink, ed. *A Parent's Guide to Childhood Obesity: A Roadmap to Health.* Elk Grove Village, Ill.: American Academy of Pediatrics, 2006.

American Cancer Society, and Edward T. Creagan. *Good For You! Reducing Your Risk of Developing Cancer.* Atlanta: American Cancer Society, 2002.

American Heart Association. *Fitting in Fitness: Hundreds of Simple Ways to Put More Physical Activity into Your Life.* New York: Clarkson Potter, 1997.

———. *The Healthy Heart Walking Book: The American Heart Association Walking Program.* New York: Macmillan Publishing Company, 1995.

———. *No-Fad Diet: A Personal Plan for Healthy Weight Loss.* New York: Clarkson Potter, 2006.

———. *6 Weeks to Get Out the Fat: An Easy-to-Follow Program for Trimming the Fat from Your Diet.* New York: Clarkson Potter, 1997.

———. *365 Ways to Get Out the Fat: A Tip a Day to Trim the Fat Away.* New York: Clarkson Potter, 1997.

———. *To Your Health! A Guide to Heart-Smart Living.* New York: Clarkson Potter, 2001.

American Medical Association. *The American Medical Association Guide to Talking to Your Doctor.* New York: Wiley, 2001.

American Medical Association and Boyd E. Metzger. *American Medical Association Guide to Living with Diabetes: Preventing and Treating Type 2 Diabetes—Essential Information You and Your Family Need to Know.* New York: Wiley, 2007.

American Psychiatric Association. *Let's Talk Facts about Eating Disorders: Healthy Minds, Healthy Lives.* Arlington, Va.: American Psychiatric Publishing, 2005.

Borushek, Allan. *2008 CalorieKing Calorie, Fat & Carbohydrate Counter.* Costa Mesa, Calif.: Allan Borushek & Assoc., 2008.

Brownell, Kelly D. *Food Fight.* New York: McGraw-Hill, 2004.

————. *The Learn Program for Weight Management.* Dallas: American Health Publishing, 2004.

Capaldi, Elizabeth D. *Why We Eat What We Eat: The Psychology of Eating.* Washington, D.C.: American Psychological Association, 2001.

Daly, Ann, Linda M. Delahanty, and Judith Wylie-Rosett. *101 Weight Loss Tips for Preventing and Controlling Diabetes.* Alexandria, Va.: American Diabetes Association, 2002.

Dellasega, Cheryl, and Charisse Nixon. *Girl Wars: 12 Strategies that Will End Female Bullying.* New York: Fireside, 2003.

Duyff, Roberta Larson, and the American Dietetic Association. *The American Dietetic Association Complete Food and Nutrition Guide.* New York: Wiley, 2006.

Gruenwald, Kate, and Amy B. Middleman. *American Medical Association Boy's Guide to Becoming a Teen.* San Francisco: Jossey-Bass, 2006.

————. *American Medical Association Girl's Guide to Becoming a Teen.* San Francisco: Jossey-Bass, 2006.

Herzog, David B., and Debra L. Franko. *Unlocking the Mysteries of Eating Disorders: A Harvard Medical School Guide.* New York: McGraw-Hill, 2007.

Kaufman, Gershen, Lev Raphael, and Pamela Espeland. *Stick Up for Yourself: Every Kid's Guide to Personal Power & Positive Self-Esteem.* Minneapolis: Free Spirit Publishing, 1999.

Lipsky, Martin S., Marla Mendelson, and Stephen Havas. *American Medical Association Guide to Preventing and Treating Heart Disease: Essential Information You and Your Family Need to Know about Having a Healthy Heart.* Hoboken, N.J.: Wiley, 2008.

McCarthy, Alice R. *Healthy Teens: Facing the Challenges of Young Lives.* 3d ed. Chicago: Bridge Communications, 2000.

McClendon, Marie, and Cristy Shauck. *The Healthy Lunchbox.* Alexandria, Va.: American Diabetes Association, 2005.

Mondimore, Francis Mark. *Adolescent Depression: A Guide for Parents.* Baltimore: Johns Hopkins University Press, 2002.

Nestle, Marion. *What to Eat.* New York: North Point Press, 2007.

Nestle, Marion, and L. Beth Dixon. *Taking Sides: Clashing Views on Controversial Issues in Food and Nutrition.* New York: McGraw Hill Contemporary Learning Series, 2003.

Rolls, Barbara J. *The Volumetrics Eating Plan: Techniques and Recipes for Feeling Full on Fewer Calories.* New York: Harper Paperbacks, 2007.

Schewe, Paul A. *Preventing Violence in Relationships: Interventions across the Life Span.* Washington, D.C.: American Psychological Association, 2002.

Shell, Ellen Ruppel. *The Hungry Gene: The Inside Story of the Obesity Industry.* New York: Grove Press, 2003.

Small Steps, Big Rewards: Walking Your Way to Better Health. Alexandria, Va.: American Diabetes Association, 2003.

Smolak, Linda, and Kevin Thompson. *Body Image, Eating Disorders, and Obesity in Youth: Assessment, Prevention, and Treatment.* Washington, D.C.: American Psychological Association, 2008.

Sothern, Melinda S., Heidi Schumacher, and T. Kristian Von Almen. *Trim Kids: The Proven 12-Week Plan that Has Helped Thousands of Children Achieve a Healthier Weight.* New York: HarperCollins, 2006.

Stricker, Paul R. *Sport Success Rₓ! Your Child's Prescription for the Best Experience.* Elk Grove Village, Ill.: American Academy of Pediatrics, 2006.

Stroebe, Wolfgang. *Dieting, Overweight, and Obesity: Self-Regulation in a Food-Rich Environment.* Washington, D.C.: American Psychological Association, 2008.

Texas Children's Hospital. *The Family Guide to Fighting Fat: A Parent's Guide to Handling Obesity and Eating Issues at the Family Table.* New York: St. Martin's Griffin, 2007.

University of New Mexico Diabetes Care Team. *101 Tips For Staying Healthy with Diabetes.* Alexandria, Va.: American Diabetes Association, 1999.

Wansink, Brian. *Mindless Eating: Why We Eat More than We Think.* New York: Bantam Books, 2007.

———. *Marketing Nutrition: Soy, Functional Foods, Biotechnology, and Obesity.* Champaign: University of Illinois Press, 2007.

Warshaw, Hope S. *Guide to Healthy Restaurant Eating.* 3rd ed. Alexandria, Va.: American Diabetes Association, 2005.

———. *Diabetes Meal Planning Made Easy.* 3rd ed. Alexandria, Va.: American Diabetes Association, 2006.

COOKBOOKS

American Cancer Society. *American Cancer Society's Healthy Eating Cookbook.* 3rd ed. Atlanta: American Cancer Society, 2005.

American Diabetes Association. *The New Family Cookbook for People with Diabetes.* New York: Simon & Schuster, 2007.

American Heart Association. *Around the World Cookbook: Low-Fat Recipes with International Flavor.* New York: Clarkson Potter, 2000.

———. *Low-Fat & Luscious Desserts: Cakes, Cookies, Pies, and Other Temptations.* New York: Clarkson Potter, 2000.

———. *The New American Heart Association Cookbook.* 7th ed. New York: Clarkson Potter, 2007.

American Medical Association. *Healthy Heart Cookbook.* Chicago: American Medical Association, 2004.

Gaines, Fabiola Demps, and Roniece Weaver. *The New Soul Food Cookbook for People with Diabetes.* Alexandria, Va.: American Diabetes Association, 2006.

Weaver, Roniece, Rojean Williams, Fabiola Demps Gaines, and Shawn Fralin. *The Family Style Soul Food Diabetes Cookbook.* Alexandria, Va.: American Diabetes Association, 2006.

INDEX